MW00952539

CHRISTIAN SKITS &

PUPPET SHOWS 5

CHRISTIAN SKITS &

PUPPET SHOWS 5

KAREN JONES

CHRISTIAN SKITS & PUPPET SHOWS 5

Copyright © 2023

Karen Jones

ISBN-13: 9798390300442

ALL RIGHTS RESERVED

Portions of this book may be copied for ministerial purposes only.

All Scriptures used in this book are from the Holy Bible, King James Version (KJV).

This cover has been designed using assets from Freepik.com and Pixabay.com.

Skits and puppet shows in this book should be undertaken with caution for the safety of the players as well as the audience. The author assumes no liability for injury or other damage to people or property as a result of the performances contained in this book.

For more information:

senoritaritaj@aol.com

Printed in the USA
Charleston, SC
www.amazon.com

TABLE OF CONTENTS

PART ONE TABERNACLE & TEMPLE PLAYS

PART TWO MODERN BIBLE CHARACTERS

PART THREE MEDLEY OF HYMNS

PART ONE

TABERNACLE & TEMPLE PLAYS

The Tabernacle, the Temple, and Me

An Easter Play

Where God Dwells

Time: 1 hour 30 minutes

Scene Descriptions and Props*

Herod's Temple

Beautiful Gate: There are two beggars sitting just outside the gate. Just inside the gate is a table where Woman 2 receives offerings such as baskets of bread, grain, wood, fruit, vegetables, and a cage of birds. The Beautiful Gate leads into the Court of the Women.

Court of the Women: The Court of the Women is the space between the Beautiful Gate and the Inner Temple Court, where the altar is located.

Temple Court: The centerpiece of the Temple Court is the altar, a perfect-square structure which can be ascended and descended with a ramp. Stairs are not permitted. There are three fires on the altar, one of which being a perpetual fire. There is a slaughter area with a table and neat piles of wood in front of the altar close to the audience. To the side of the altar closest to the Sanctuary is the laver (a large basin for ceremonial washing).

The Temple Sanctuary: The Temple proper or Sanctuary consists of three areas: the entrance hall, the Holy Place, and the Holy of Holies (Most Holy Place). There is a door or gate between the entrance hall and the Holy of Holies which must be unlocked every morning and locked every evening. A veil separates the Holy Place and the Holy of Holies (Most Holy Place). This building in our scenes lacks a side wall so the audience can view the interior.

The Entrance Hall

The entrance hall contains features which are noteworthy. On each side of the hall, there are built-in niches where knives are stored. There are also two tables which serve a special purpose in the Temple. A marble table is on the right side of the gate or door which leads to the Holy Place and a gold one on the left. Every Sabbath, 12 freshly-baked loaves of unleavened bread are brought into the Temple to replace those of the previous week on the table of showbread. The freshly baked showbread may be set on the marble table to cool; however, the showbread on the gold table of showbread is considered to have a higher level of sanctity. Once the sacred bread is placed on the gold table of showbread, it can never be "demoted" by being placed on a lesser table, i.e., the marble table. For this reason, the week-old showbread can only be moved to the gold table before being eaten by the priests.

*Sources found in the back of the book.

The Holy Place

The Holy Place—the larger area of the Sanctuary—houses the menorah, the table of showbread, and the incense altar. Twelve loaves of unleavened bread and two bowls of frankincense are on the table of showbread, where they would have remained for a week. On the Sabbath, another 12 loaves will be brought in to replace these and sprinkled with the frankincense. The remaining frankincense will remain on the table with the new loaves. The old 12 loaves will be moved to the gold table in the entrance hall and subsequently will be eaten by the Priests. The frankincense that was on the table with the old loaves will be burned on the incense altar before the priests eat the loaves. The supplies needed for the menorah are a gold oil flask, a gold oil lamp, gold tongs to remove the spent wicks, and a gold receptacle to hold the ashes and spent wicks.

Holy of Holies

Beyond the large veil, the Holy of Holies is empty. In the previous Temple (Solomon's Temple, also called the First Temple), the Holy of Holies held the Ark of the Covenant, but this was either hidden by priests, or stolen or destroyed by the Babylonians when the First Temple was razed in 586 or 587 BC.

The House of Immersion: The House of Immersion was under the actual Temple. Priests shuttle to and from this place daily to cleanse themselves prior to service in the Temple. Next to the pool is a fire where the Priests warm themselves. White towels are also needed. In Scene 1, the Priests will go to the right side of the audience to the House of Immersion.

The Jordan River: This is the location where John the Baptist baptizes Jesus. It's on the left side of the audience.

Benjamin's House: Benjamin's house consists of one room with a woodshed attached. Inside the room is a dinner table with four chairs. Next to the fireplace there is a rocking chair or armchair and a side table. This is where Sapphire will sew. She needs swatches of cloth, needles, and thread. Sapphire's bronze mirror and an oil lamp are on the table. Beulah will wash dishes and needs a wash basin and several pots.

There is a cot at the side of the room where Ishmael will be placed after an accident in a cave. At the end of the cot is a chest where the model of the Tabernacle will be stored in Scene 3. The model Tabernacle needs the majority of the holy furniture, such as the altar, the bronze laver, the menorah, the table of showbread, incense altar, and the Ark of the Covenant. A miniature High Priest is needed as well.

The woodworking shop is attached to the house. Inside, there is a woodworking table. A censer (which is used by priests in the Temple) is hanging on the wall. There are random woodworking tools. A small table is upturned on the woodworking table, to be repaired in the first scene. There is a shovel and a pick leaning against a wall. Benjamin will whittle in a scene, so he needs a piece of wood and a knife.

The Tomb Scene: There are three tombs. One is for Ishmael. The second one houses Dead Man and Dead Woman. The third one is for Jesus. Each of the "dead" people should exit with a linen sheet draped around his or her shoulders.

Golgotha: There are three crosses, two of which have thieves hanging on them. One cross is lying on the ground. Guard 3 will offer Jesus the cup of "vinegar." A sponge or cloth to dip in the vinegar and a long stick are also needed.

Cast Descriptions and Props*

NARRATOR:	The narrator speaks throughout the play. He may be in modern-day clothes or dressed in a tunic or robe of a common townsperson.
PRIESTS:	The priests work in Herod's Temple. They wear the same clothing: tunics or robes, pants, belts, and turban head coverings. Priests cannot be in the Temple without a head covering. There are at least nine priests, not including Ephraim and Benjamin.
BENJAMIN:	Benjamin is a father, husband, and Levitical priest. He also does carpentry and has a woodworking shop attached to his house. He is in his 40s or 50s. He only wears priestly attire in the Temple.
BEULAH:	Beulah is Benjamin's wife. She is in her 40s or early 50s.

*Sources found is in the back of the book.

SAPPHIRE: Sapphire is the oldest child of Benjamin and Beulah. She is an older teen. She sews. Her props include a mirror, needles, thread, and scraps of cloth.

ISHMAEL: Ishmael is the son of Benjamin and Beulah. He is a teen around 15 years of age. He is of slight build, because he will need to be carried during one scene. His best friend is Samuel.

Ishmael is fascinated by a model of the Tabernacle of Moses that he and his father are working on together. As the play progresses, Ishmael will receive the bronze altar, the bronze laver, the Ark of the Covenant, and the High Priest figurine. By the end of the play, all the holy furniture will be in the model Tabernacle, including the menorah, the table of showbread, and the table of incense. Ishmael uses a bag with a shoulder strap to take bread to the beggars at the Temple gate.

EPHRAIM: Ephraim is a father and Levitical priest. He wears priestly attire only in the Temple.

SAMUEL: Samuel is Ephraim's son and Ishmael's best friend. He is a teen. He carries an animal-skin bag with a shoulder strap.

JERUSALEM CHOIR: The Jerusalem Choir consists of worshippers at the Temple. They should be dressed as common townspeople wearing colored tunics, sashes, and sandals. Men and women can wear head coverings. Men must wear head coverings in the Temple. Man 1, Man 2, Man 3, Woman 1, Woman 2, Husband, and Wife are all part of the Choir. Twelve or more people would be optimal.

MAN 1:   He is one of the townspeople who are outspoken when approaching the Jordan River and in the Temple. He can be any age. He is related to the Dead Man and embraces him when the latter is resurrected.

MAN 2:   He is one of the townspeople who are outspoken in the Temple. He can be any age. He is related to the Dead Woman and embraces her when she is resurrected.

MAN 3:   He is one of the townspeople who are outspoken in the Temple. He can be any age.

WOMAN 1:   She is one of the townspeople who are outspoken when approaching the Jordan River. She can be any age. She is related to the Dead Man and embraces him when he is resurrected.

WOMAN 2:   She is one of the townspeople. She sits just inside the gate at a table of supplies that have been given to the Temple. She is related to the Dead Woman and embraces her when she is resurrected.

HUSBAND: Husband and wife are bringing peace offerings to the Temple. He is in his 30s. He and his wife have been trying to have a baby for 10 years.

WIFE: Husband and wife are bringing peace offerings to the Temple. She is in her 30s. She and her husband have been trying to have a baby for 10 years.

JESUS: Jesus is wearing normal clothing like that of the other townspeople. His clothing is ripped and bloodied in scene 4.

JOHN THE BAPTIST: John is the cousin of Jesus. He baptizes Jesus. John is dressed like the other townspeople but more ragged or rough and worn.

JAMES: James is a disciple of Christ. He is dressed like the other townspeople. When he goes inside the Temple, he needs to wear a head covering.

JOHN THE APOSTLE: John is a disciple of Christ. He is dressed like the other townspeople. When he goes inside the Temple, he needs to wear a head covering.

| **MALAK:** | Malak is a blind man who sits by the Beautiful Gate. Jesus heals him. Once Malak is healed, he can join the Jerusalem Choir. |

MALAK: Malak is a blind man who sits by the Beautiful Gate. Jesus heals him. Once Malak is healed, he can join the Jerusalem Choir.

TOBEY: Tobey is a lame man who sits by the Beautiful Gate. Jesus heals him. Once Tobey is healed, he can join the Jerusalem Choir.

RICH YOUNG RULER: The rich young ruler is a young man who approaches Jesus to ask how he can achieve eternal life. His clothing should be fancier, perhaps with a gold-colored sash and turban.

DEAD MAN: The dead man is in a tomb and comes back to life when Jesus is crucified. The dead man should be wrapped in grave clothes. Man 1 and Woman 1 are related to the dead man and embrace him after he is resurrected.

DEAD WOMAN: The dead woman comes back to life when Jesus is crucified. She should be wrapped in grave clothes. Man 2 and Woman 2 are related to her and embrace her after she is resurrected.

GUARDS: The Roman guards are wearing helmets, segmented armor breastplates, tunics, belts, and sandals. They are carrying swords and whips. Guards 1 and 2 crucify Jesus. Guard 3 is watching over the 2 thieves and has the cup of vinegar.

2 THIEVES: The thieves are on the crosses. They are dressed like the other townspeople, but their clothing has been ripped and bloodied.

MARY: Mary is the mother of Jesus. She is dressed like the other townspeople.

Scene 1
Purification
Time: 28 minutes

Scenes: House of Immersion, Jordan River, the Temple, BENJAMIN's house
Cast: (28+) 5 PRIESTS including PRIEST 1 and PRIEST 2; EPHRAIM; NARRATOR; JOHN THE BAPTIST; JESUS; the JERUSALEM CHOIR, consisting of townspeople including MAN 1 and WOMAN 1; ISHMAEL; BENJAMIN; SAMUEL; SAPPHIRE; BEULAH; LAME BEGGAR TOBEY; BLIND BEGGAR MALAK; WOMAN 2 at the gate; HUSBAND; WIFE
Songs: "Wade in the Water," "Is Your All on the Altar?"
Props: House of Immersion: a fire, white towels
Temple: tin cups for the BEGGARS, sheep 1, basin of water to wash sheep 1, table of supplies (baskets of bread, wood, vegetables, a cage with birds), sheep 2, sheep bleating sound effect, platter of unleavened bread loaves, silver bowl to catch sheep 2's blood, sheep breast and shoulder, baskets with fruit, vegetables, spices, or breads for several townspeople in the JERUSALEM CHOIR
BENJAMIN's house: swatches of cloth, table with loose legs, tools, incense censer, Tabernacle model (with model bronze altar, bronze laver, and Ark of the Covenant), animal-skin bag with shoulder strap with "spices" inside for SAMUEL, bag with shoulder strap for ISHMAEL with two loaves of bread, SAPPHIRE's bronze mirror, loaf of bread for BEULAH

(The Temple PRIESTS and EPHRAIM are going down to purify themselves in the House of Immersion. EPHRAIM immerses himself first. The other PRIESTS watch. They warm themselves by the fire waiting for the song "Wade in the Water" to begin before they immerse themselves.)

NARRATOR: It's predawn on this beautiful day in Jerusalem. The priests are up early as usual to purify themselves in the House of Immersion before heading to their duties on the Temple Mount.

(On the other side of the stage, JOHN THE BAPTIST enters from behind the audience with JESUS following behind.)

11

NARRATOR:	More than a mile away at the Jordan River, we can see John the Baptist just arriving. He has a little spring in his step this morning. In a few days he will reach the age of 30, which is a special time for anyone in the Levitical family line. As is the custom, John the Baptist will follow in his father's footsteps and make his way to the Temple to show himself to the priests to be commissioned for service.

JOHN THE BAPTIST: *(Shouting as he is walking in)* I am the voice of one calling in the wilderness. *(Motions forward with one hand)* Make straight the way for the Lord.

JESUS: *(Motions to the Jordan River)* John, I think now would be the perfect time for you to baptize me since we're here at the Jordan River.

JOHN THE BAPTIST: Me? *(Shakes his head in protest)* No, my Lord, I can't baptize You. I am not worthy to untie Your shoes. You should baptize me.

(MAN 1 and WOMAN 1 enter behind the audience.)

MAN 1: Look! There's Jesus and John the Baptist.

WOMAN 1: *(Calls to the JERUSALEM CHOIR TOWNSPEOPLE offstage behind the audience.)* Let's go to the Jordan.

(MAN 1 and WOMAN 1 rush to the riverside.)

JESUS: It needs to be done, John, to fulfill all righteousness. It will be an example to all of My followers. *(Motions to the TOWNSPEOPLE as they enter)*

JOHN THE BAPTIST: I understand. *(Nods his head)* Yes, my Lord, what You say I will do.

(The JERUSALEM CHOIR trickles in a few at a time to watch the baptism, positioning themselves on either side of the river. JESUS is still talking to JOHN, who nods in

agreement. Simultaneously, three events are taking place during the following song: the PRIESTS start to go down to the House of Immersion and immerse themselves in the water one by one; JOHN is baptizing JESUS; and EPHRAIM is drying off, going to the Temple, and retrieving sheep 1 in the Temple. As each PRIEST immerses himself, he comes up wiping at his face, grabs a white towel to dry off, and then goes over to the Temple.)

JERUSALEM CHOIR:	*(Sings "Wade in the Water")* Wade in the water. Wade in the water, children. Wade in the water. God's gonna trouble the water.
PRIESTS:	See that host all dressed in white. God's gonna trouble the water. The leader looks like the Israelite. God's gonna trouble the water.
JERUSALEM CHOIR:	Wade in the water. Wade in the water, children. Wade in the water. God's gonna trouble the water.

(JESUS and JOHN get into the Jordan River. JOHN raises his hands as if in prayer as JESUS prepares to be baptized. JOHN then baptizes JESUS. JESUS and a PRIEST in the House of Immersion go down simultaneously, and both come out of the water with hands upraised. Also at the same time as JESUS' baptism, EPHRAIM uses the basin of water to wash sheep 1.)

PRIESTS:	If you don't believe they've been redeemed, God's gonna trouble the water. Just follow Jesus down to Jordan's stream. God's gonna trouble the water.
JERUSALEM CHOIR:	Wade in the water. Wade in the water, children. Wade in the water. God's gonna trouble the water.

(JOHN and JESUS get out of the water. JESUS dries His face with His head covering.)

NARRATOR: Only in hindsight would the townspeople of Jerusalem realize the significance of John the Baptist baptizing Jesus. Having been raised around the Temple, they would have known that only a Levitical priest could wash and inspect the sacrifice to ensure that it was without spot or blemish.

(The curtains close for the House of Immersion scene and the Jordan River scene. The House of Immersion scene will be changed to the Golgotha scene. The Jordan River scene will be changed into the tomb scene. BENJAMIN's house scene opens.)

Now, let's take a peek into a priest's home in Jerusalem. We find Benjamin the Levite in his woodworking shop. He's not on duty this week, so he's free to work at his regular job as a carpenter.

(SAPPHIRE is in BENJAMIN's house sitting in the rocking chair sewing. BENJAMIN is standing behind a worktable in the woodworking shed. There is a small, upturned table on top of it, and BENJAMIN is tightening the legs. ISHMAEL enters holding the Tabernacle model.)

ISHMAEL: Father, what are you working on?

BENJAMIN: The widow Dinah asked me to repair her table. Why are you up before dawn?

ISHMAEL: I could barely sleep last night after we made the model of the Tabernacle. I'm so excited to work on the holy furniture and vessels. Do you think you will have time today to work on it?

BENJAMIN: Maybe I can find some time. *(Smiles at his son)*

(ISHMAEL sets the Tabernacle down and holds up the bronze altar from the outer court.)

ISHMAEL: Father, why was the altar in the Tabernacle and Solomon's Temple made of bronze, but today in Herod's Temple it's made of hewn stone?

14

BENJAMIN: Well, in Moses' day, the Tabernacle had to be moved from place to place. They couldn't carry around the huge altar we have today. The altar in the Tabernacle was made of acacia wood; but what do you think would happen to an altar made of wood?

ISHMAEL: It would burn with the sacrifice, so that's why it was overlaid with bronze.

BENJAMIN: Exactly. When Herod had our new Temple built, he made a permanent structure with stones that will withstand the heat. *(Takes the bronze altar model from ISHMAEL)* But do you know why the altar had four horns?

ISHMAEL: Oh, sure. I've seen enough sacrifices to know that the horns are needed to tie down the lamb or other animals.

BENJAMIN: That's the practical purpose, but there's more. The Scriptures say in the book of Psalms, "Jehovah is my strength, and my fortress, and my deliverer; my God, my rock; I will trust in Him; He is my shield, and the horn of my salvation, my high tower." *(Touches one of the horns on the altar)* The horn of my salvation.

ISHMAEL: I don't understand, Father. How can God be the horn of our salvation?

BENJAMIN: Isaiah prophesied about a coming Messiah, saying, "He was oppressed and afflicted, yet he did not open his mouth; he was led like a lamb *(motions to the altar again)* to the slaughter . . ."

ISHMAEL: *(Pauses in contemplation)* Are you saying the coming Messiah will be sacrificed like a lamb on the altar?

BENJAMIN: That's my understanding of the Scripture.

ISHMAEL: I can't comprehend how that could ever happen. I would imagine the Messiah will be guarded and protected. There's certainly no way we, as a people, would allow our Messiah to be slaughtered,

15

ISHMAEL: would we, Father?

BENJAMIN: I've thought about that a lot, Ishmael. Perhaps if most Jews did not
                     see the signs and if they did not believe when the Messiah arrived.

ISHMAEL: Do you think *we* will know the Messiah when we see Him?

BENJAMIN: I think we will, son. If we have faithful hearts, we will know Him.

*(SAMUEL enters. He is wearing an animal-skin bag crossed over his body. Some sprigs
of plants are sticking out to indicate spices. SAMUEL knocks on the doorframe before
entering the woodworking shed.)*

                     Well, hello, young man.

ISHMAEL: Hey, Samuel!

SAMUEL: Hello, sir. *(To ISHMAEL)* Ishmael.

BENJAMIN: What brings you by today? *(Hands the bronze altar back to
                     ISHMAEL and returns to work on the table)*

SAMUEL: Sir, as you know, my father is serving in the Temple this week.

BENJAMIN: Yes, indeed.

SAMUEL: He is hoping to be chosen to offer up the incense. *(Points to a
                     censer hanging on the wall)*

BENJAMIN: Yes, all the priests hope to be the one chosen to offer up a
                     pleasing aroma to the Lord. It is the most coveted duty at the

BENJAMIN: Temple. *(Holds up one finger)* It's an honor that a priest is
                     allowed to do only once in his lifetime, so it's very special.

ISHMAEL: Have you ever been chosen to offer incense?

BENJAMIN: Not yet. *(Joyfully)* Son, when I am chosen to offer incense, you will know it. I will shout all the way home at the end of the week.

ISHMAEL: I would be honored to be chosen to take out the ashes or refill the laver with water. I wish I could sneak in there and perform some priestly duties. I feel like I'll never be old enough to be a priest.

BENJAMIN: *(Shaking his head no)* Be patient, my son. When you are 25, you can start joining me on our family's week of service to watch and learn. Then, at 30 years old, you will be commissioned, and you will be able to join the ranks of priests just like all the other Levites. Your desire to work for the Lord's house is a good thing, but your ambition must be tempered with obedience to God's Holy Word. Everything must be done in order.

SAMUEL: You don't want to end up like Korah, Dathan, and Abiram when they rebelled against Moses and Aaron in the desert. They wanted to offer incense and sacrifices, too.

BENJAMIN: Yes, they were Levites of age, so they didn't understand why only Moses and Aaron were able to perform certain holy duties. Korah and the others accused Moses and Aaron of setting themselves up higher than the other Levites, when it was really God who had set them apart.

ISHMAEL: I remember that story. Korah brought 250 men to offer incense to God at the gate of the Tabernacle.

BENJAMIN: *(Picks up the censer and swings it slowly)* So here they were with their censers. On the outside it looked innocent, as if they just wanted to do a service for the Lord; but God knew their rebellious hearts. The anger and animosity they had for Moses and Aaron was like a tumor growing deep in their souls. Samuel, do you remember what happened to Korah and the others?

SAMUEL: *(Opens his arms wide)* The earth opened up and swallowed them.

BENJAMIN: And the 250 other men who came to burn incense?

SAMUEL: They were burned with fire.

ISHMAEL: *(Takes the censer from his FATHER)* I remember Moses took all 250 of the censers and hammered them out flat and fitted them on the altar.

BENJAMIN: *(Takes the censer back and returns it to its spot on the wall)* Yes, son. It's better to nail your ambitions to the altar before they lead to destruction.

ISHMAEL: Don't worry, Father. I have a desire to work for the Lord, but I want to be in God's will. I don't want to be rebellious like the Israelites in the desert.

BENJAMIN: Samuel, see that model of the Tabernacle of Moses that Ishmael has?

SAMUEL: Yes, sir.

BENJAMIN: Ishmael and I worked for hours yesterday making that. *(To ISHMAEL)* Last night after you went to bed, I continued working. *(Pulls out a model of the Ark of the Covenant and hands it to ISHMAEL. ISHMAEL gasps.)*

ISHMAEL: The Ark of the Covenant! Thank you, Father. I love it.

BENJAMIN: You're welcome. Let me quiz you two scholars. What was inside the Ark of the Covenant while it was in the Tabernacle?

ISHMAEL: First of all, the two stone tablets where Moses wrote the Ten Commandments.

SAMUEL: And a pot of manna that God provided for the Israelites to eat in the desert.

BENJAMIN:	And don't forget Aaron's rod. Do you remember after Korah and the others were destroyed? The Israelites were angry with Moses and Aaron. They had doubts. So God instructed Moses to get one rod from each of the 12 tribes of Israel to represent their clans. The tribes wrote the name of their tribe on the rods. On the Levites' rod, they wrote the name of Aaron. Then Moses placed the rods with the Ark of the Covenant in the Holy of Holies.
ISHMAEL:	And the next morning, Aaron's rod had budded and brought forth fruit.
SAMUEL:	But the others hadn't.
BENJAMIN:	Exactly. God made it very clear to the others whom He had chosen. And that's why Aaron's rod was kept in the Ark of the Covenant; to warn against rebellion. I get so excited when I talk about the service of the Lord. I apologize, Samuel. You didn't come here for a history lesson.
SAMUEL:	It's OK, sir. Ishmael and I talk about it all the time, but the reason I came by today is because *(holds up the animal-skin bag)* my mother wants me to take this bag of spices over to the Temple before they start their duties. I was hoping Ishmael could come along with me.
ISHMAEL:	May I, Father?
BENJAMIN: **BENJAMIN:**	Sure. *(Motions to the Tabernacle model)* We will work on your Tabernacle later. Go tell your mother where you are going so she won't worry.
ISHMAEL:	Yes, sir. *(To SAMUEL as he rushes out with the model Ark of the Covenant in hand)* I'll be right back.

(ISHMAEL enters the house scene, where his sister, SAPPHIRE, is sewing.)

Sapphire, where's Mother?

SAPPHIRE:	She was gone when I woke up. I think she went to check on Grandmother and Grandfather.
ISHMAEL:	When she comes back will you tell her I'm going with Samuel to the Temple?
SAPPHIRE:	I'll tell her. *(Points to the Ark of the Covenant)* Whatcha got there?
ISHMAEL:	Father made me the Ark of the Covenant for my Tabernacle model. *(Shows it to SAPPHIRE)* What do you think it was like to go into the Holy of Holies before the Babylonians destroyed the Temple?
SAPPHIRE:	The Shekinah Glory filled the place! Oh, Ishmael. Father said it had to be the most amazing experience. It saddens me when we pass by the Temple because I know the Holy of Holies is empty now.
ISHMAEL:	One day I hope to be the one to find the Ark of the Covenant and restore it to its rightful place in the Holy of Holies. Where do you think it is today?
SAPPHIRE:	I don't know, Ishmael. Father said the Babylonians could have destroyed it, or perhaps a wise priest hid it away in a cave when he saw the army invading.
ISHMAEL:	I hope it was hidden. I'm going to look for it one day. I'm going to explore all the caves around here.
SAPPHIRE:	I believe if anyone can find the Ark of the Covenant, it's you. *(Gets up, puts two loaves of bread in a bag with a shoulder strap, and hands it to ISHMAEL)* Give this to the two beggars at the Beautiful Gate.
ISHMAEL:	*(Smiling proudly)* I will. Thanks, Sis. I'll see you later. I've got to go.
SAPPHIRE:	OK, see you later.

(ISHMAEL runs back to the woodworking shed, places the Ark of the Covenant in the Tabernacle model, and picks it up.)

ISHMAEL: *(To SAMUEL)* Let's go. *(He and SAMUEL rush away to the Temple.)*

(BENJAMIN takes the repaired table off the woodworking table. He sticks his head in the door to speak to SAPPHIRE.)

BENJAMIN: I fixed the widow Dinah's table. Tell your mother I'll be home before supper.

SAPPHIRE: Yes, Father.

(Carrying the table, BENJAMIN exits in the opposite direction of the Temple. SAPPHIRE sets her sewing down and stands up. She raises her head and hands toward heaven.)

SAPPHIRE: *(Praying)* God, my family comes from the line of Aaron. My brother wants more than anything to be a High Priest one day if that is Your will. His desire to be in the Holy of Holies will probably come true. Perhaps the Ark of the Covenant will be found in his lifetime, and he will feel Your Shekinah Glory. *(Pauses)* I know I should not covet, Lord. Please forgive me, but I want to be in Your presence, too. My soul longs to be near You. It's all I've ever wanted.

(SAPPHIRE's MOTHER, BEULAH, enters with a loaf of bread in her hand.)

BEULAH: Sapphire, I'm home.

SAPPHIRE: *(Wipes at her eyes)* I'm here, Mother. I was just praying. Ishmael wanted me to let you know he went to the Temple with Samuel. And Father is delivering the widow Dinah's table.

BEULAH: What are the boys doing at the Temple? Talking to the scribes?

SAPPHIRE: I'm not sure, Mother, I forgot to ask.

21

BEULAH: No harm done.

(SAPPHIRE sits down, still in deep contemplation, and picks up her sewing again.)

                     Sapphire? Are you OK?

SAPPHIRE: Who am I, Mother? *(Throws her arms up in the air questioningly)* What is my purpose? What do I have to offer God?

BEULAH: So many questions for such a young girl. Why are you asking such things? Has something happened?

SAPPHIRE: No, I just don't see how I fit into God's master plan. Ishmael has plans to find the Ark of the Covenant and become a High Priest. Father is a priest. He performs many of the duties that are so very important in the Temple. You care for all of us and our grandparents. What about me?

BEULAH: Don't compare yourself to others, Sapphire. You mustn't measure your worth by another person's achievements. You'll never have peace that way. God made you for a specific purpose, and I know for a fact, one reason is to praise Him.

SAPPHIRE: Yes, I can praise Him, but if the Ark of the Covenant is found and placed back in the Holy of Holies, Ishmael will be able to feel the Shekinah Glory. I'm a girl. I can't be a High Priest and go into the Holy of Holies.

(BEULAH opens her bag and pulls out a miniature bronze laver. SAPPHIRE sets her sewing on the table next to her.)

BEULAH: Your grandmother donated one of her old bronze mirrors so Ishmael could have this laver for his model Tabernacle.

SAPPHIRE: Oh, Mother. Ishmael is going to be so excited to have the laver. He got up early this morning to work on it with Father.

BEULAH: Do you know who supplied the bronze to make the laver in the Tabernacle?

SAPPHIRE: No.

BEULAH: It wasn't the great leaders of the tribes of Israel. Just like with Ishmael's laver, it was women who provided the bronze. The women who served at the gate of the Tabernacle gave Moses their bronze mirrors. Without the laver, the priests couldn't do their duties.

SAPPHIRE: Why did they use mirrors to make the laver?

(BEULAH picks up SAPPHIRE's bronze mirror from the side table and hands it to SAPPHIRE.)

BEULAH: What do you see?

SAPPHIRE: *(Looks into the mirror)* Me. My reflection.

BEULAH: Exactly. The bronze mirrors were formed into the laver, and then the laver was filled with water. *(BEULAH puts her hands in front of SAPPHIRE's mirror.)* So when the priests were washing their hands and feet, they could see their reflections in the shiny bronze surface.

SAPPHIRE: I suppose it helped them see any spots or stains.

BEULAH: It did. They could inspect themselves closely, and then the water cleansed every spot. That's what we all must do: inspect our hearts closely for any impurity.

(BEULAH pauses. SAPPHIRE stands up and takes the laver from her MOTHER.)

You and your brother are at ages when you are wondering what you will do with your lives and how you will serve God with purpose. All God wants is for us to give Him of ourselves. Nothing

| BEULAH: | more and nothing less. Give your all to God in whatever your hands find to do. In that you will find your purpose. |

| SAPPHIRE: | There's nothing I want more than to worship God in His presence. I feel like I should sacrifice more. I just feel like nothing I do is enough. |

| BEULAH: | Oh, it's enough, Sapphire. You may not be the one trimming lamps in the Holy Place or offering sacrifices on the altar, but there's a psalm that says, "The sacrifices of God are a broken spirit: a broken and a contrite heart, O God, thou wilt not despise." God loves a heart that seeks after Him, Sapphire. |

(The Temple scene opens, and the JERUSALEM CHOIR individuals are praying and/or milling about the perimeter of the Temple area. Some are holding baskets with fruit, vegetables, spices, or breads. BLIND BEGGAR MALAK and LAME BEGGAR TOBEY are sitting on one side of the gate holding tin cans. WOMAN 2 is sitting at a table just inside the gate. There are supplies such as baskets of bread, wood, vegetables, and a cage with birds. A HUSBAND brings sheep 2, and a tearful WIFE brings a platter with unleavened bread to EPHRAIM and PRIESTS 1 and 2, to be offered as a peace offering.)

| NARRATOR: | At the Temple, we see an Israelite couple who, after praying for a child for 10 years, finally conceived. They are bringing a peace offering to thank God for His goodness to their family. Let's watch as this magnificent ceremony is performed. |

| EPHRAIM: | Once the child is born, you will need to bring two turtledoves, but for now you are so delighted by our God's provisions that you want to give this free-will offering. |

| HUSBAND: | Yes, we want to show God our gratefulness. |

| EPHRAIM: | What you do is a good thing. God will be pleased. |

(BEULAH starts to sing to SAPPHIRE.)

24

BEULAH: *(Sings "Is Your All on the Altar?")*
You have longed for sweet peace,
And for faith to increase,

(The HUSBAND places his hand on sheep 2's head as PRIEST 1 mimes slaughtering it. Then EPHRAIM places a silver bowl under the sheep's neck to catch blood.)

And have earnestly, fervently prayed.

(The WIFE is raising her platter of unleavened loaves as she cries and worships. The HUSBAND places an arm around the WIFE. He is praying and raising his other hand in worship. Sheep 2 is taken off to be dismembered by PRIESTS 2 and 3 with their backs to the audience. The JERUSALEM CHOIR individuals are worshipping as well, raising their hands and praying.)

But you cannot have rest
Or be perfectly blest
Until all on the altar is laid.

JERUSALEM   *(Chorus)*
CHOIR: Is your all on the altar of sacrifice laid?
Your heart does the Spirit control?

(EPHRAIM splashes the blood on the altar.)

You can only be blest
And have peace and sweet rest
As you yield Him your body and soul.

(PRIEST 1 continues to butcher sheep 2 with his back to the audience as PRIESTS 2 and 3 turn around with the shoulder and breast in their hands. PRIEST 2 hands the shoulder to the HUSBAND and guides him in heaving or waving it before the altar as PRIEST 3 waves the breast before the Lord. The HUSBAND returns the shoulder to PRIEST 2 and then takes the breast from PRIEST 3. He waves it as well, as PRIEST 2 continues waving the shoulder and the WIFE waves or heaves the unleavened bread. Some of the worshippers wave their arms back and forth, mimicking the PRIESTS' back-and-forth motion.)

BEULAH: Would you walk with the Lord
                    In the light of His Word,
                    And have peace and contentment alway?
                    You must do His sweet will
                    To be free from all ill;—
                    On the altar your all you must lay.

JERUSALEM   *(Chorus)*
CHOIR: Is your all on the altar of sacrifice laid?
                    Your heart does the Spirit control?
                    You can only be blest
                    And have peace and sweet rest
                    As you yield Him your body and soul.

(Some of the worshippers bend and bow their bodies in worship, mimicking the PRIESTS' up-and-down motions.)

BEULAH: Oh, we never can know
                    What the Lord will bestow
                    Of the blessings for which we have prayed,
                    Till our body and soul
                    He doth fully control
                    And our all on the altar is laid.

JERUSALEM   *(Chorus)*
CHOIR: Is your all on the altar of sacrifice laid?
                    Your heart does the Spirit control?
                    You can only be blest
                    And have peace and sweet rest
                    As you yield Him your body and soul.

(The JERUSALEM CHOIR disperses gradually. The PRIESTS stay at their posts and busy themselves with duties around the altar area, such as adding wood or putting away the bowl and knife. BENJAMIN's house scene closes.)

Scene 2
Miracles
Time: 22 minutes

Scenes: The Temple, BENJAMIN's house
Cast: (25+) NARRATOR; ISHMAEL; SAMUEL; LAME BEGGAR TOBEY; BLIND BEGGAR MALAK; WOMAN 2 at the gate; 5 PRIESTS; EPHRAIM; JERUSALEM CHOIR including MAN 1, MAN 2, MAN 3; JESUS; JAMES; JOHN THE APOSTLE; RICH YOUNG RULER
Song: "Jesus Is Here Right Now" (with adaptations)
Props: Temple: tin cans for BEGGARS; supplies for WOMAN 2's table such as baskets of bread, wood, vegetables, and a cage with birds; ISHMAEL's model of the Tabernacle and bag with two loaves of bread; SAMUEL's animal-skin bag with "spices"; silver altar rakes and shovels for PRIEST EPHRAIM and the other PRIESTS
BENJAMIN's house: High Priest figure sized to fit in the Tabernacle model

(The JERUSALEM CHOIR individuals are mingling in and around the Temple. Some are praying. Some are worshipping. Some are in groups chatting. PRIEST EPHRAIM and a couple of other PRIESTS are tending to the fire on the altar using silver shovels and rakes.)

NARRATOR: Ishmael and Samuel make their way to the Temple, which is already bustling with activity.

(ISHMAEL and SAMUEL enter walking to the Temple. ISHMAEL is carrying his Tabernacle model and has a bag over his shoulder with the bread while SAMUEL is carrying the bag of spices. The LAME BEGGAR TOBEY and the BLIND BEGGAR MALAK are sitting close to the gate of the Temple with tin cans. They lift them from time to time calling for alms.)

TOBEY: Alms. Alms.

ISHMAEL: Good morning, Mr. Tobey. It's going to be a nice day, I do believe.

TOBEY: Yes, Ishmael. It's a glorious morning.

(ISHMAEL opens his bag and pulls out the bread SAPPHIRE gave him.)

MALAK: Alms, please.

ISHMAEL: Don't worry, Mr. Malak, my sister told me to bring you both some bread.

MALAK: Thank you. *(Starts to eat the bread)*

TOBEY: Thank you, young man. *(Eating the bread hungrily)* Send your parents and sister my regards. Your family is always so kind to me.

ISHMAEL: I will indeed.

(SAMUEL notices his father, EPHRAIM, carrying a silver altar rake close to the altar.)

SAMUEL: Oh, there's my father. *(Calls out)* Father!

(SAMUEL rushes off to his father. ISHMAEL pats MALAK on the shoulder, then follows SAMUEL. The boys both make sure their heads are covered if inside the Temple area. EPHRAIM moves away from the altar area, closer to the Women's Court.)

EPHRAIM: Yes, son.

SAMUEL: Mother told me to bring these spices *(pats his bag)* to the Temple.

EPHRAIM: That's fine, son. Give them to the woman at the gate. I need to get back to my duties.

SAMUEL: Yes, sir.

(SAMUEL and ISHMAEL make their way back toward the gate. EPHRAIM returns to the altar.)

(JESUS, JAMES, and JOHN THE APOSTLE enter and approach the Temple. ISHMAEL

nudges SAMUEL and motions toward JESUS and the others, who are approaching the BEGGARS MALAK and TOBEY.)

TOBEY:	*(Holds up his tin cup)* Alms.
MALAK:	*(Holds up his tin cup)* Alms. Alms.
TOBEY:	Alms.
JESUS:	*(Pauses to look at the BEGGARS)* How long have you been in this condition?
TOBEY:	My whole life, sir. Do you have any water?
JESUS:	Are you thirsty?
TOBEY:	Yes, I am.
JESUS:	I have Living Water, My child. If you drink of My water, you will never thirst again. *(To MALAK)* What about you? How long have you been in this condition?
MALAK:	I was born blind, my Lord.
JESUS:	Do you want to be whole?
MALAK:	Whole?
JESUS:	Yes, do you want to see? *(To TOBEY)* And you, child, do you want to be quenched of your thirst?
TOBEY:	You speak of strange things. You are Jesus of Nazareth, aren't You?
JESUS:	I am.
MALAK:	Yes, I know Your voice. I hear You speaking in the Temple daily.

29

TOBEY: Oh, Jesus, Son of David, have mercy on me. Forgive my sins.

JAMES: Not today, beggars. Let's go, Jesus.

(JAMES and JOHN THE APOSTLE continue to walk into the Temple, making sure their heads are covered. They talk among themselves, but JESUS remains.)

MALAK: Please don't pass us by, Jesus.

TOBEY: I know You are able to heal me.

(JESUS bends over and touches TOBEY on the head.)

JESUS: Get up. Take up your bed and walk. Your sins are forgiven.

(TOBEY examines his legs. He stretches out his legs, springs to his feet, and starts running.)

TOBEY: I can feel my legs!

(JESUS places his hands over MALAK's eyes.)

JESUS: You are healed. Purify yourself and then go show yourself to the priest.

(MALAK closes and then opens his eyes.. He gasps.)

MALAK: *(Starts out quietly)* I can see. *(He holds his hands in front of his face.)* I can see. I can see!!

(MALAK embraces JESUS. Then he looks around in awe at all of creation that he has never seen. ISHMAEL and SAMUEL clap and celebrate with them as the townspeople, the JERUSALEM CHOIR, clamor around. TOBEY returns to JESUS and jumps up and down, showing JESUS he is healed. The JERUSALEM CHOIR worships, congratulates, and starts to sing "Jesus Is Here Right Now" as MALAK and TOBEY go to the audience and tell random people they were healed. PRIEST EPHRAIM hears the ruckus and comes to see from a distance what is going on. He watches skeptically. Everyone worships as

the JERUSALEM CHOIR sings. JESUS walks around, greets, and even prays for people.)

JERUSALEM CHOIR:	*(Sings to the tune of "Jesus Is Here Right Now"* Jesus is here right now; reach out and touch Him. Jesus is here right now; help you'll receive. Jesus is standing so near; ready your heart to cheer. Jesus is here right now; only believe.
MALAK:	*(Singing)* I was born blind and hopeless; I sat begging all day. I had no way out of my plight; each day was the same. But Jesus passed by my way, and He listened to me. Just a few words were spoken, and now I can see. *(Shouts and goes off worshipping)*
JERUSALEM CHOIR:	*(Singing)* Jesus is here right now; reach out and touch Him. Jesus is here right now; help you'll receive. Jesus is standing so near; ready your heart to cheer. Jesus is here right now; only believe.
TOBEY:	*(Singing)* I felt empty for years; I was suffering in pain. My life was a desert place, just aching for rain. But Jesus showed up in my life and forgave my sin. He said, "I have living water for you; you won't thirst again."
JERUSALEM CHOIR:	*(Singing)* Jesus is here right now; reach out and touch Him. Jesus is here right now; help you'll receive. Jesus is standing so near; ready your heart to cheer. Jesus is here right now; only believe.

(The JERUSALEM CHOIR immediately disperse and start doing what they would usually do in and around the Temple. JESUS, JAMES, and JOHN THE APOSTLE go into the Temple with their heads covered. Some of the JERUSALEM CHOIR gather around to hear JESUS speak. SAMUEL and ISHMAEL, holding his Tabernacle model, rush to JESUS as well.)

ISHMAEL:	Hosanna to the Son of David.

SAMUEL:	Hosanna to the Son of David.
BOTH BOYS:	Hosanna to the Son of David.
MAN 1:	Go away, kid.
MAN 2:	Yeah, scram!
EPHRAIM:	Son, what are you doing? *(In contempt to JESUS)* Do you hear what these children are saying?
JESUS:	Yes. Have you never read, "From the mouths of children and infants You have ordained praise?"
EPHRAIM:	You speak blasphemy!

(PRIEST EPHRAIM shakes his head, sighs, and walks back to resume his duties. He passes by JAMES and JOHN THE APOSTLE.)

You need to do something about your Teacher. He is causing an uproar around the Temple. The High Priest doesn't like all this commotion.

(JAMES and JOHN THE APOSTLE go back out with JESUS. JAMES grabsISHMAEL's arm while JOHN does the same to SAMUEL, escorting them away.)

JOHN THE APOSTLE:	Let's go. The Master is busy.
JESUS:	Wait, James. Let the little children come to Me, and do not hinder them! For the kingdom of heaven belongs to such as these.

(JAMES and JOHN THE APOSTLE release the children. JESUS pulls them close. ISHMAEL places the Tabernacle model on JESUS' lap.)

What is this?

ISHMAEL: It's a model of the Tabernacle, just like Moses and the Israelites had when they wandered in the desert.

JESUS: Yes, I see. *(JESUS holds it up.)* The Tent of Meeting. Where did you get such a great piece of workmanship?

ISHMAEL: My father helped me make it. He's a carpenter. It was very difficult because the acacia wood is twisted and thorny. It was hard to use.

JESUS: *(Nods his head knowingly)* God can use the most difficult material and *(looks around at everyone)* the most difficult people. *(Looks closely at the Tabernacle)* Even though the building material was difficult to use, you and your father did a fine job, a very fine job. Did you know that acacia wood is virtually indestructible?

ISHMAEL: Yes, my father said it is very strong and you can't tell how rough it is when it's covered with gold.

JESUS: Ahh yes, the gold. The acacia wood is like the flesh, and the gold is like God. God can make the roughest sinner gleam like the sun.

ISHMAEL: Wow.

JESUS: You and I have something in common, young man. My earthly father was a carpenter, too. I spent a lot of time with him crafting furniture and other things. *(Points to the model of the Tabernacle)* There's so much to be learned from this. Think of the similarities between a tent of acacia wood and cloth in the desert, a temple of stone in here in Jerusalem, *(motions around to the Temple)* and a Temple of flesh prophesied by the prophets. What do these three things have in common?

MAN 1:   What do you mean, Master? What is the Temple of flesh?

JESUS: *(Hands the Tabernacle model back to ISHMAEL and stands up. He stretches out His arms on either side.)* Destroy this temple, and in

JESUS:	three days I will raise it up again.
MAN 2:	This Temple *(motions around to the Temple)* took 46 years to build, and if it's destroyed, You think You are going to raise it up in three days?
MAN 1:	Impossible.
MAN 3:	He's talking in riddles.

(Individuals in the JERUSALEM CHOIR start arguing with MEN 1, 2, and 3, and a huge commotion starts. JAMES and JOHN THE APOSTLE usher JESUS out of the Temple. ISHMAEL motions for SAMUEL, and the two follow JESUS.)

JAMES:	The Temple is so beautiful, Master. Look at the majesty of it.
JESUS:	Yes, but there will come a day when it will no longer stand. Every stone will be thrown down.
JAMES:	But, Lord . . .

(The RICH YOUNG RULER rushes to JESUS and falls at his feet.)

RICH YOUNG RULER:	Good Master, what shall I do that I may inherit eternal life?

(JESUS bends down and lifts up the RICH YOUNG RULER.)

JESUS:	Young man, you know the commandments: do not commit adultery, do not kill, do not steal, do not bear false witness, defraud not, honor your father and mother?
RICH YOUNG RULER:	Master, I've kept all these commandments from my youth.
JESUS:	*(Places a hand on the YOUNG RULER's shoulder)* There's one thing you haven't done. Go sell everything, give it to the poor, and then you'll have your treasure stored up in heaven. Come take up

JESUS:	your cross and follow Me.
RICH YOUNG RULER:	Sell everything? *(Pauses. Looks around. Shakes his head and throws up his hands)* But . . . *(Turns around dejectedly and walks off)* You just have no idea. . . .

(As the RICH YOUNG RULER walks away, JESUS looks back at the JERUSALEM CHOIR people still talking.)

JESUS:	I think I need to go find a quiet place.
JAMES:	Yes, let's go.

(JESUS, JAMES, and JOHN THE APOSTLE exit with some following after them. The Temple scene closes with ISHMAEL and SAMUEL outside the Temple. BENJAMIN's house scene opens.)

ISHMAEL:	Samuel, I know now!
SAMUEL:	What? What do you know?
ISHMAEL:	I know Jesus is the Messiah. I'll see you later. I have to go talk to my father.
SAMUEL:	I'll see you around, Ishmael. *(Waves and scurries out)*

(ISHMAEL waves and runs off holding his Tabernacle model. He runs to his house, where BENJAMIN, BEULAH, and SAPPHIRE are sitting at the table. ISHMAEL bursts through the door, excited about his revelation.)

ISHMAEL:	Jesus of Nazareth is the Messiah!

(BENJAMIN and BEULAH are startled and bolt up from the table, unsure what's wrong.)

BEULAH:	What, son?
BENJAMIN:	What?

ISHMAEL: *(Places the Tabernacle model on the table)* Jesus of Nazareth is the Messiah! I just know it! Today, Jesus came to the Temple. The blind man Mr. Malak and the crippled beggar Mr. Tobey were there like always at the Beautiful Gate. And Jesus healed them! *(Grabs BEULAH's hands)* I saw it with my own eyes, Mother!

BENJAMIN: Slow down, son. What are you talking about?

ISHMAEL: Father, remember you told me if we have faithful hearts when the Messiah comes we will know who He is? Well, I watched Jesus of Nazareth heal a blind man and a lame man. It was the most spectacular thing I've ever seen, Father.

(BEULAH gasps and puts her hand over her mouth.)

BEULAH: Malak, the blind man? The man who has sat at the gate of the Temple for more than 20 years?

ISHMAEL: He's not blind anymore!

(BEULAH turns to BENJAMIN.)

BEULAH: I told you this was the rumor in the Women's Court at the Temple. They all said they had heard about Jesus turning water into wine at a wedding in Cana.

BENJAMIN: Tell us what happened, son.

ISHMAEL: This morning, Samuel and I went to give spices to the Temple, and the blind man and the lame man were sitting there just like every other day, begging. Sapphire gave me bread for them. *(Goes over to SAPPHIRE and sits next to her)* They were so hungry, Sapphire. They ate it as soon as I gave it to them and told me to thank the family.

BENJAMIN: Get back to the healing.

ISHMAEL: Jesus walked by and asked them both how long they had been in their conditions. He asked them if they wanted to be healed.

SAPPHIRE: Did they say yes?

ISHMAEL: They both said yes, and then Jesus touched them. You should have seen it. The lame man jumped to his feet and started shouting. *(Springs from his chair reenacting the LAME MAN's healing)* I've never seen someone jump up so fast. He was running, telling everyone. Then the blind man wiped at his eyes. *(Wipes at his own eyes and reenacts the BLIND MAN's healing)* He screamed out, "I can see! I can see!"

BEULAH: Was Samuel's father there?

ISHMAEL: He was.

BENJAMIN: What did he think?

ISHMAEL: He didn't seem too thrilled. Father, why don't some of the priests like Jesus?

BENJAMIN: I think it's because He stirs everybody up when He's around. I think they like to maintain the status quo.

BEULAH: There's no status quo with Jesus. The last time Sapphire and I went to the Temple, He caused quite the ruckus.

SAPPHIRE: He flipped tables over and drove the moneychangers out with a whip, but I don't blame Him. Those guys come in there and sell the sacrificial animals for very high prices. They cheat the people. It made Jesus angry.

ISHMAEL: I wish I had seen that. *(Makes whipping motions as if he's casting someone out of his house)*

BENJAMIN: Stay here for a minute, Ishmael. I have something for you that is perfect for this moment.

(BENJAMIN retrieves a box and opens it. He pulls out a miniature High Priest that will fit in the model Tabernacle.)

ISHMAEL:	Is that the High Priest?
BENJAMIN:	It is.
ISHMAEL:	Thank you, Father! I love it. But what does the High Priest have to do with what we are talking about?
BENJAMIN:	*(Picks up the model Tabernacle)* Everything in the Tabernacle is a type or shadow from which we can learn important lessons.
ISHMAEL:	What does the High Priest symbolize?
BENJAMIN:	I will answer your question with a question. What does the High Priest do in the Holy of Holies on Yom Kippur?
ISHMAEL:	He sprinkles blood and makes sure our sins are covered. *(Thinks for a moment, then gasps as he realizes the connection)* Just like the Lamb that is led to slaughter!
SAPPHIRE:	Just like the Messiah!
BEULAH:	The Messiah is our High Priest.
BENJAMIN:	Yes, He will atone for our sins. Ishmael, should we go to the shop and work on the menorah and the table of showbread?
ISHMAEL:	Yes, let's go. Father, this is a day I will never forget!

(BENJAMIN and ISHMAEL walk toward the woodshed as the curtain is closed.)

Scene 3
Trim Your Wick
Time: 22 minutes

Scenes: BENJAMIN's house, the Temple, Tomb scene
Cast: (28+) NARRATOR, ISHMAEL, SAMUEL, PRIESTS 1–9, JESUS, JAMES, JOHN THE APOSTLE, the JERUSALEM CHOIR, BENJAMIN, BEULAH, SAPPHIRE, EPHRAIM
Songs: "God Is So Good" (with adaptations), "I Need Thee Every Hour"
Props: BENJAMIN's house: scroll, whittling knife and wood for BENJAMIN, chest, Tabernacle model and contents, model of the menorah, pot and washcloth for BEULAH, sewing swatches and a cloth to wipe the table for SAPPHIRE, shovel, pick, cloths to wash ISHMAEL, stretcher to carry ISHMAEL, blanket
Temple: gold flask of olive oil, gold oil lamp, gold tongs to remove wicks, a gold receptacle to hold the spent wicks, fake flame, basket of fish and bread for JESUS, 4 gold platters of 6 loaves of bread (12 loaves already on the table of showbread and 12 more to replace those), 4 bowls of frankincense, smoke machine, fake fire for the menorah, incense altar, perpetual fire on the outer altar

| NARRATOR: | Three years later. |

(The curtains open on BENJAMIN's house and the Temple scene. In BENJAMIN's house, ISHMAEL and SAMUEL are inside. ISHMAEL is sitting on his bed. SAMUEL is sitting at the table reading a scroll. At the same time, PRIEST 1 is in the Temple. He has the gold flask of olive oil in his hand. The gold oil lamp to transfer the flame from the perpetual fire to the menorah, the gold tongs to remove the spent wicks, and the gold receptacle to hold the spent wicks, and more wicks are already in the Holy Place. None of the wicks are burning on the menorah. He sets the gold oil flask on the second stair of the menorah and goes about working on removing the old wicks and cleaning out the ashes. There is a perpetual fire burning in the Temple Court.)

Ishmael has grown serious and determined. His model of the Tabernacle has long since been completed. He spends hours every

NARRATOR: day studying the Scriptures with his friend Samuel, but there's still a spark inside of him that wants adventure.

(ISHMAEL gets up and sits next to SAMUEL. SAMUEL passes the scroll to him.)

ISHMAEL: *(Reading from the scroll)* "Make a joyful noise unto the LORD, all ye lands. Serve the LORD with gladness: come before his presence with singing. Know ye that the LORD he is God: it is he that hath made us, and not we ourselves; we are his people, and the sheep of his pasture. Enter into his gates with thanksgiving, and into his courts with praise: be thankful unto him, and bless his name." *(Stops reading and taps his fingers on the table)*

SAMUEL: What is it?

ISHMAEL: *(Points at the scroll and repeats the verse)* "Serve the LORD with gladness."

SAMUEL: When we are 25, we can start training in the Temple.

ISHMAEL: That's another seven years. I'm so tired of everyone treating us like we are still children. *(Pauses)* Do you remember back when we were younger and that rich young ruler came to talk to Jesus?

SAMUEL: Yes.

ISHMAEL: How old do you think he was?

SAMUEL: Probably not much older than we are now.

ISHMAEL: Jesus didn't tell him to wait until he was 25 to train and 30 to serve Him.

SAMUEL: You're right. Jesus told him to sell everything he had right then. *(Pauses)* What are you thinking?

ISHMAEL: *(Stands up)* We saw Jesus heal that blind man and the lame man. We have listened to Him teach in the Temple so many times over the last few years. I know without a doubt that He is the Messiah. I

ISHMAEL: want to follow Him. There's no reason I shouldn't be able to. I'm old enough to make my own decisions.

SAMUEL: That's true.

ISHMAEL: *(Leans over and opens a chest at the foot of the cot. He picks up his Tabernacle model, holds it up for a look.)* Remember when Father and I made this?

SAMUEL: I do.

(ISHMAEL stares at the model quietly and sits back down on the side of the cot.)

     What is it, Ishmael?

ISHMAEL: What if I never have the opportunity to work in the Temple?

SAMUEL: *(Stands up and walks over to ISHMAEL)* Why would you say such a thing, Ishmael?

ISHMAEL: *(Shrugs)* I don't know. There are just times when I feel like I'll never get to fulfill my dream.

(SAMUEL bends and takes the model menorah out of the Tabernacle.)

SAMUEL: Don't be hopeless and impatient, Ishmael. My father told me a story about the menorah. He said sometimes the priests go in and all the wicks are burning brightly. Other days only a couple of the wicks are burning.

ISHMAEL: What do they do?

(PRIEST 1 leaves the Holy Place and heads to the altar with the gold oil lamp.)

SAMUEL: The priest will use the light from the other wicks to light the ones that are out. My father said that's why it's so important to have people in your corner. When you are feeling like your light has been snuffed out, they can light your wick. But then there are days

SAMUEL: when the priest enters the Holy Place and none of the wicks are burning. There will be days when even your best friends can't encourage you. Ever feel that way?

ISHMAEL: Yes, Samuel. I'm sorry. You're a great friend, but today I'm discouraged. My wick has definitely burned out.

SAMUEL: But that's not the end of the story. On the days when all the wicks are out, they don't just close the doors of the Temple and shut the place down.

ISHMAEL: What do they do?

(PRIEST 1 retrieves a fake flame with the gold oil lamp and heads back to the Holy Place.)

SAMUEL: God has provided a perpetual fire on the altar. The priest goes outside to the altar and takes a flame from the fire that's always burning to light the menorah. God provides the light.

(ISHMAEL nods his head in realization. PRIEST 1 is lighting the menorah with the light from the perpetual fire.)

ISHMAEL: That reminds me of the prophet Jeremiah's words, "But *his word* was in mine heart as a burning fire shut up in my bones, and I was weary with forbearing, and I could not *stay.*"

SAMUEL: That's powerful!

(ISHMAEL stands, takes the menorah from SAMUEL, and puts it back into the Tabernacle. He slaps SAMUEL on the shoulder.)

ISHMAEL: I've been thinking a lot, and I have an idea.

SAMUEL: What?

ISHMAEL: When the Babylonians destroyed the Temple, *(takes out the Ark of the Covenant and holds it up)* the Ark of the Covenant

ISHMAEL: disappeared. It was either destroyed or carried away, or it may have been hidden by a priest somewhere around Jerusalem.

SAMUEL: Right.

ISHMAEL: I think people will take me . . . us . . . more seriously if we are the ones to find it.

SAMUEL: *(Laughs)* We've been talking about searching for the Ark since we were children, but we've never done more than look under a few rocks.

ISHMAEL: I'm serious about it now, Samuel.

SAMUEL: Where would you go to look?

ISHMAEL: I've thought about it a lot over the years. *(Puts the menorah back in the Tabernacle and places the model back in the chest at the foot of the cot)* I think I've narrowed it down to a couple of caves around here. You know about Zedekiah's cave, right?

SAMUEL: Sure, everyone knows that cave.

ISHMAEL: Well, it's so close to the Temple. I think the priests smuggled the Ark of the Covenant deep inside there. We may have to dig into the walls of the cave, but I think we could find it. Should we go?

SAMUEL: Now?

ISHMAEL: There's no time like the present. It'll be an adventure, like when we were kids.

SAMUEL: *(Shrugs)* It goes against my better judgment, but if it will make you feel better, I'll do it. Can you imagine what Jesus would think if we found the Ark of the Covenant?

ISHMAEL: He might ask us both to be His disciples. Let's go find a pick and a shovel.

43

(ISHMAEL and SAMUEL go to BENJAMIN's woodshed and get a pick and shovel. They then rush offstage toward Zedekiah's cave. Both scenes remain open. JESUS, JAMES, JOHN THE APOSTLE, and the JERUSALEM CHOIR enter from the right side of the audience.)

JESUS: *(As He reaches the front of the audience with the DISCIPLES)* We should find some food. *(Points in the distance)* We still have a long way to go. The people will be hungry soon.

(Everyone gathers in front of the audience. There are two trays of six loaves of unleavened bread on the table of showbread and two bowls of frankincense. PRIESTS 2 through 5 enter the Holy Place and stand near the table of showbread.)

JAMES: We should send all the people away so they can find something to eat.

JESUS: No, let's not send them away.

JOHN THE   *(Picks up a basket of fish and bread)* Jesus, some women brought
APOSTLE: these fish and loaves.

(PRIESTS 6 and 7 enter the entrance hall of the Temple, each carrying a tray of six small loaves of unleavened bread. PRIESTS 8 and 9 are following behind, each holding a bowl of frankincense. They place the showbread and bowls of frankincense on the marble table in the entrance hall to the right of the door or gate of the Holy Place. In the Holy Place, PRIESTS 2 and 3 take the frankincense off the table of showbread and go stand near the altar of incense. PRIESTS 4 and 5 stand ready to take off the two platters of unleavened bread. PRIESTS 6 through 9 enter with the fresh bread and 2 new bowls of frankincense. As PRIESTS 4 and 5 are sliding the platters of unleavened bread off the table of showbread in one direction, PRIESTS 6 and 7 slide their platters on to ensure that there is always showbread on the table. PRIESTS 8 and 9 sprinkle the new loaves with frankincense and then set the bowls of frankincense on the table. PRIESTS 4 and 5 take the old showbread out to the entrance hall and set them on the gold table. PRIESTS 2 and 3 burn the old frankincense on the incense altar. A little smoke rises to show something is being burned.)

JESUS: Give it to me.

(JOHN THE APOSTLE hands JESUS the basket. JESUS holds the basket up.)

Bless this food for the nourishment of these people.

(JESUS hands the basket to JAMES and JOHN THE APOSTLE.)

NARRATOR: As the disciples prepare to pass out the bread and fish, the priests gather in the Temple as is the custom on every Sabbath.

In Leviticus the Scripture states, "Take the finest flour and bake twelve loaves of bread. This bread is to be set out before the LORD regularly, Sabbath after Sabbath, on behalf of the Israelites, as a lasting covenant. It belongs to Aaron and his sons, who are to eat it in the Sanctuary area, because it is a most holy part of their perpetual share of the food offerings presented to the LORD."

As long as the Temple stood, the priests continued to replace the bread on the table of showbread and eat the bread in the presence of the Lord. The bread signified that God would supply His people with sustenance, both physical and spiritual, while they were doing His service.

(The old loaves of showbread are passed out to the PRIESTS. At the same time, JAMES and JOHN THE APOSTLE pass out the bread to the JERUSALEM CHOIR.)

PRIESTS,
JESUS, JAMES
& JOHN THE
APOSTLE:

(Sing to the tune of "God Is So Good")
Come take this bread.
Eat, eat your fill.
Come take this bread.
Eat your fill and be fed.

JERUSALEM
CHOIR:

Feast from above,
Gift from God's hand,
Sent here with love
To save God's Holy Land.

(The Temple scene closes. JESUS, JAMES, and JOHN THE APOSTLE continue to hum the song and eat bread as they exit the opposite side of the audience that they entered.)

45

(In BENJAMIN's house, BENJAMIN, BEULAH, and SAPPHIRE enter as everyone exits the Temple scene. SAPPHIRE starts wiping the dinner table as BEULAH begins to wash a pot. BENJAMIN sits in the rocking chair next to the end table and picks up a whittling knife and a piece of wood. He starts whittling. Some of SAPPHIRE's sewing work is on the end table. There is a stretcher on the cot covered with a blanket.)

BENJAMIN: I've talked to Elazar. Do you remember him?

SAPPHIRE: Yes, he's in charge of the veil at the Temple, right?

BENJAMIN: You're right. And there are 82 girls who make two veils every year. If the one hanging in front of the Holy of Holies gets dirty, it gets replaced with a new one. I've noticed recently your stitchwork has really improved.

SAPPHIRE: *(Confused)* What are you saying, Father? Do you think I could be one of the girls who sew at the Temple?

BENJAMIN: I certainly think it's a possibility. *(Pauses, then gets up and looks outside)* It's getting late.

(Suddenly EPHRAIM rushes in from behind the audience holding ISHMAEL in his arms, assisted by SAMUEL. BEULAH drops the pot and wipes her hands on her robe.)

BENJAMIN: What's going on?

EPHRAIM: There's been an accident.

BENJAMIN: *(In shock)* Beulah!

(BEULAH rushes to BENJAMIN, and the two start to reach for ISHMAEL.)

EPHRAIM: Don't touch him, Benjamin. You can't touch a dead body. You would be unclean.

SAPPHIRE: Dead?! Mother, what's going on?

BENJAMIN: The Scriptures say I can touch my own son's body.

(Everyone helps place ISHMAEL's body on the bed. BEULAH throws herself over ISHMAEL.)

BEULAH: My baby! What happened to my baby?

BENJAMIN: Let me check him, Beulah. Let me see.

(BENJAMIN pulls BEULAH back and examines ISHMAEL. He checks his pulse and listens to his chest. He moves ISHMAEL's head from side to side and opens an eye. Then he places his hand on ISHMAEL's head and bows his head. SAPPHIRE, realizing her brother is really dead, lets out a cry, and BEULAH throws herself over ISHMAEL again.)

BEULAH: *(Wails)* My baby!

(SAPPHIRE goes to her MOTHER's side and puts her hand on her MOTHER's back. BENJAMIN stands upright and goes over to EPHRAIM and SAMUEL.)

BENJAMIN: What happened to our boy?

(SAMUEL lowers his head.)

SAMUEL: I'm so sorry, sir. *(Starts to cry)*

EPHRAIM: Samuel and Ishmael went to Zedekiah's cave today.

SAMUEL: To look for the Ark of the Covenant. I knew we shouldn't.

EPHRAIM: They ended up deep inside, and apparently there were some falling rocks.

SAMUEL: Big rocks fell all around us, Mr. Benjamin. One hit Ishmael on the head, and he never got back up. *(Starts to cry again. BENJAMIN hugs the boy.)* I just wanted to help him feel better. I shouldn't have encouraged him. It's all my fault.

EPHRAIM: It was a horrible accident, Benjamin. We are terribly sorry. *(He pulls SAMUEL away from BENJAMIN and hugs his son.)*

(BENJAMIN goes over to the bed. He falls to his knees next to the chest. He opens the chest and pulls out the Tabernacle model. He hugs it close.)

BENJAMIN: There was so much more I wanted to teach you. So much more you needed to know. I needed more time.

SAPPHIRE: *(Falls to the floor next to her FATHER and speaks through her tears)* No, Father. He already knew the most important thing. He knew the Messiah.

BENJAMIN: *(To EPHRAIM)* You touched my son. I'm sorry you are unclean now, Ephraim.

EPHRAIM: *(Waves away BENJAMIN's concern)* God will understand.

(EPHRAIM and a weeping SAMUEL are led out, and they exit. SAPPHIRE stands up, lifts her hands to heaven, and starts to sing "I Need Thee Every Hour.")

SAPPHIRE: *(Sings)*
                      I need Thee, oh, I need Thee;
                      Ev'ry hour I need Thee;
                      Oh, bless me now, my Savior,
                      I come to Thee.

(BENJAMIN places the model of the Tabernacle on the table, then he and BEULAH use a cloth to wash ISHMAEL to prepare him for burial. The JERUSALEM CHOIR start to come to view the body, a couple at a time, some bringing food. Some linger and comfort the family. BENJAMIN motions toward ISHMAEL and then shows them in. The Tomb scene opens.)

SAPPHIRE: *(Sings)* I need Thee ev'ry hour,
                      Most gracious Lord;
                      No tender voice like Thine
                      Can peace afford.

JERUSALEM CHOIR:	*(Sings chorus of "I Need Thee Every Hour")* I need Thee, oh, I need Thee; Ev'ry hour I need Thee; Oh, bless me now, my Savior, I come to Thee.
SAPPHIRE:	I need Thee ev'ry hour, Stay Thou nearby; Temptations lose their pow'r When Thou art nigh.
JERUSALEM CHOIR:	*(Chorus)* I need Thee, oh, I need Thee; Ev'ry hour I need Thee; Oh, bless me now, my Savior, I come to Thee.
SAPPHIRE:	*(While SAPPHIRE is singing, the JERUSALEM CHOIR is preparing to carry ISHMAEL on the stretcher to the tomb.)* I need Thee ev'ry hour, In joy or pain; Come quickly and abide, Or life is vain.
JERUSALEM CHOIR:	*(Sing the chorus while entombing ISHMAEL with his family following)* I need Thee, oh, I need Thee; Ev'ry hour I need Thee; Oh, bless me now, my Savior, I come to Thee.
NARRATOR:	The family placed Ishmael in a tomb. As was the custom, Benjamin and his family purified themselves three days after laying their beloved to rest and once again on the seventh day, allowing them once again to go to the Temple.

(The JERUSALEM CHOIR exits. Lights dim.)

49

Scene 4
The Veil
Time: 18 minutes

Scenes: BENJAMIN's house, the Temple, Tomb scene, Golgotha
Cast: (38+) NARRATOR, BEULAH, SAPPHIRE, 9 PRIESTS including PRIEST 1 and 2, BENJAMIN, JESUS, 3 GUARDS, MARY, 2 THIEVES on the crosses, DEAD MAN, DEAD WOMAN, ISHMAEL, JERUSALEM CHOIR including MAN 1, MAN 2, WOMAN 1, WOMAN 2, HUSBAND, WIFE
Song: "I Surrender All" (with adaptations)
Props: BENJAMIN's house: sewing swatches for SAPPHIRE
Temple: sheep 3, gold cup, sheep bleating sound effects, a pole on which to tether the sheep, thunder sound effect
Golgotha: whip, long stick, sponge or cloth, hammer, stakes or nails, sheep bleating sound effect, thunder sound effect

(In the dimness, BEULAH is sitting with her head on the table. SAPPHIRE is in the rocking chair sewing. The lights come back on, and the Temple scene opens as well. Simultaneously, BENJAMIN is in the Temple. He is watching as PRIESTS 1 and 2 bring in sheep 3 for sacrifice. The other PRIESTS are tending to the altar and helping with the sheep.)

NARRATOR:	Several weeks later, Ishmael's family is trying to put the pieces of their lives back together; however, people deal with grief in different ways. Some isolate themselves, while others throw themselves into their work. We find Benjamin in the Temple. It's his clan's assigned week to serve, and he is preparing the sacrifice. His wife, Beulah, is grieving. She isn't coping well with her loss.
SAPPHIRE:	What can I do for you, Mother?

(BEULAH and SAPPHIRE are alone in their home. BEULAH is weeping with her head down on the table. SAPPHIRE looks at her MOTHER.)

50

BEULAH: *(Lifts her head and shakes her head no)* Nothing, Sapphire.

SAPPHIRE: Will you eat if I cook?

BEULAH: I can't, dear, I'm sorry.

SAPPHIRE: Please, Mother. I feel like I'm losing you, too.

BEULAH: I've lost all hope, Sapphire. *(Weeping)* A mother shouldn't have to bury her son.

SAPPHIRE: *(Pauses and looks up to heaven)* Remember when Ishmael saw Jesus heal the blind man and the lame man?

BEULAH: My baby was so impressed. *(Puts her head back down on the table and cries)* My baby! My life is over!

SAPPHIRE: Mother, please don't say that. *(Sets her sewing down and goes over to embrace her MOTHER)* If Jesus can open blind eyes and make lame legs walk, surely He can heal a broken heart and give hope to the hopeless. Wait here, Mother. I know who can help you.

(SAPPHIRE rushes out to the left of the audience, and the house scene goes dark. BEULAH remains at the table with head down. Golgotha scene opens. GUARD 3 is in the scene watching two THIEVES on their crosses. GUARDS 1 and 2 lead a beaten and bloody JESUS in on the right side of the audience. MARY follows behind. They push and shove Him until they reach Golgotha. MARY watches with her hand over her mouth in anguish.)

NARRATOR: Sapphire will search for Jesus, but she doesn't know that Jesus' time has come. On the other side of town, another mother is about to lose her son as well.

(GUARDS 1 and 2 shove JESUS down to the ground. They start striking him with a whip. JESUS reacts to each blow. The GUARDS "nail" JESUS to the cross. Simultaneously at the Temple, PRIEST 1 takes a sheep. While JESUS is being strapped to the cross, PRIEST 2 ties sheep 3 to a pole where it will soon be slaughtered.)

51

NARRATOR: They beat Jesus and took Him to the Place of the Skull, a hill called Golgotha, to be crucified.

(JESUS is lifted up on the cross as SAPPHIRE rushes into the scene.)

SAPPHIRE: Where's Jesus? I need to find . . . *(Stops when she sees JESUS on the cross)*

NARRATOR: As is the custom, Priest Benjamin gives the lamb a cup of water before it is sacrificed while the guards are offering Jesus a drink as well on Golgotha. Matthew 27:34 says, "They gave him vinegar to drink mingled with gall: and when he had tasted thereof, he would not drink." Jesus knew that the drink was meant to dull the pain, so He refused, choosing instead to feel every ounce of agony for the redemption of the world.

(While the NARRATOR is speaking, BENJAMIN takes a gold cup and gives the sheep water to drink. At the same time, GUARD 3 lifts up a sponge or cloth on a stick and touches JESUS' mouth. After it touches His mouth, He turns His head in refusal. SAPPHIRE runs up to JESUS and grabs hold of his legs.)

SAPPHIRE: Jesus, my family needs You. Please help us. *(SAPPHIRE looks up at JESUS, and He gazes down at her with compassion.)*

(A rumbling sound, the thunder sound effect, is heard.)

BENJAMIN: *(Looks up acknowledging the thunder but continues)* Kill the sacrifice.

(BENJAMIN puts his hand on the head of the sheep while PRIEST 1 mimes cutting its throat. They turn and quickly take it to a table and work on cleaning it with their backs turned.)

JESUS: It is finished! *(JESUS bows His head in death.)*

(Lights flicker. Sounds effects of thunder can be heard. There's a shaking. SAPPHIRE is torn away from JESUS. The JERUSALEM CHOIR rushes in. Some of them go to Golgotha, some to the Temple. Chaos ensues.)

NARRATOR: Matthew 27:50–54 says, "Jesus, when he had cried again with a loud voice, yielded up the ghost. And, behold, the veil of the temple was rent in twain from the top to the bottom; and the earth did quake, and the rocks rent." *(There is shaking in the Temple. The veil rips in two and falls to the ground. BENJAMIN braces himself and looks around in disbelief as he covers his head. Everyone runs and covers themselves. The large stones in front of the tombs start to shake.)* "And the graves were opened;" *(The large stones fall away from the tombs.)* "and many bodies of the saints which slept arose," *(Several of the dead exit the tomb, including DEAD MAN, DEAD WOMAN, and ISHMAEL. They pull off their grave linens and examine themselves.)* "and came out of the graves after his resurrection, and went into the holy city, and appeared unto many." *(ISHMAEL and other DEAD walk toward the Temple. MAN 1 and WOMAN 1 embrace DEAD MAN. MAN 2 and WOMAN 2 embrace DEAD WOMAN. They all celebrate together.)* "Now when the centurion, and they that were with him, watching Jesus, saw the earthquake, and those things that were done, they feared greatly, saying, . . ."

GUARD 1: Truly this was the Son of God.

(Commotion is happening all around—individuals of the JERUSALEM CHOIR are running, embracing, and rushing to and fro. BENJAMIN comes out of the Temple and sees ISHMAEL in the distance. The remaining PRIESTS exit as well looking around at the commotion.)

BENJAMIN: Who is . . . that? *(Squints and turns his head for a better look, not believing his eyes)* Is that—? No. It can't be.

ISHMAEL: Father!

BENJAMIN: Ishmael?

ISHMAEL: Father! *(Runs to BENJAMIN and falls into his arms)* The Messiah came to me while I was in my grave and told me to wake up. He wants me to live for Him.

BENJAMIN: Oh, Ishmael! My son. That's exactly what we will do.

(SAPPHIRE gets to her feet and stares at JESUS.)

SAPPHIRE: I came here to ask You to help my family. I don't know what has happened, but I know You have done something that will save my family. *(She rushes toward the Temple and sees BENJAMIN and ISHMAEL at the same time. She shrieks.)* Ishmael! *(Runs to ISHMAEL, and the two embrace.)* Ishmael! I knew Jesus did something. I knew it!

ISHMAEL: Sapphire, Jesus healed me and wants me to follow Him.

SAPPHIRE: I knew Jesus did something for our family. Mother is sick with grief. We must go to her. Look. *(Points in the distance)*

(BEULAH exits her house and starts walking slowly in grief toward the Temple, trying to figure out what the commotion is all about. BEULAH cannot believe her eyes. She stops dead in her tracks and stares at her family. The JERUSALEM CHOIR starts to calm down and move to the side, leaving space for BEULAH and ISHMAEL.)

BEULAH: That boy looks just like my son. *(Looks heavenward)* God, this sorrow is too much for me to bear.

(ISHMAEL sees his mother in the distance.)

ISHMAEL: There's Mother. *(With sadness in his voice)* Oh, Mother. I am here.

BEULAH: Ishmael? *(Still not moving, she wipes at her eyes in disbelief.)*

ISHMAEL: It's me, Mother. Jesus of Nazareth brought me back to follow Him.

(SAPPHIRE runs to BEULAH and points to ISHMAEL.)

BEULAH: Can it be? God, have you heard my prayers?

ISHMAEL: He has, Mother. He has!

BEULAH: Oh, Ishmael! *(She runs to ISHMAEL and puts her hand on his face.)*

ISHMAEL: Please don't grieve any more, Mother. I am here. I'm so sorry I caused you pain.

(BEULAH falls into ISHMAEL's arms. SAPPHIRE hugs her FATHER.)

                    Father, remember when you and I made the Tabernacle of Moses?

BENJAMIN: Of course I do, son.

ISHMAEL: When I was younger, I showed it to Jesus. He lifted it up and asked me a question I was unable to answer, but now I think I know.

BENJAMIN: What did He ask?

ISHMAEL: He asked me what the Tabernacle of Moses, the Temple in Jerusalem, and His Temple of flesh had in common.

BENJAMIN: He often spoke in parables. What do you suppose was the answer?

ISHMAEL: I believe the Tabernacle housed the Presence of God. The same with the Holy of Holies in the Temple, and God was in Him also. .

BENJAMIN: I believe you are exactly right. That reminds me of the most amazing thing that happened today in the Temple.

SAPPHIRE: What, Father?

BENJAMIN: Do you know the veil that kept sinful man out of the presence of God?

SAPPHIRE &
ISHMAEL: Yes.

BENJAMIN: It's there no longer.

SAPPHIRE: What do you mean?

55

BENJAMIN: I was in the Temple, and I heard it. The whole place shook, and the veil ripped from top to bottom and fell to the ground.

ISHMAEL: What do you think that means?

BENJAMIN: I believe it means that the High Priest is no longer the only one who can be in the presence of God. Jesus has opened the door to whosoever will.

SAPPHIRE: Even me, Father?

(BENJAMIN holds SAPPHIRE's face in his hands.)

BENJAMIN: Anyone! Even you!

                   (Sings to the tune of "I Surrender All" verse one)
                   All the quaking, all the shaking,
                   Then the veil was torn in two;
                   Not reserved just for the High Priest;
                   (Sings to SAPPHIRE and ISHMAEL)
                   We can be in His presence, too.

SAPPHIRE: We must go thank Jesus.

(The family, arm in arm, goes to JESUS. During this song, the JERUSALEM CHOIR worships and/or kneels.)

BENJAMIN: *(Sings refrain. When they reach JESUS, BENJAMIN falls to his knees.)* I fall down at Your feet; I fall down at Your feet.
                   Finally I'm in Your presence.
                   I fall down at Your feet.

SAPPHIRE &   *(Sing to the tune of "I Surrender All" verse two)*
ISHMAEL: I always longed for Your presence,
                   But for me it couldn't be.
                   In Your loving and Your kindness,
                   You robed Yourself in humanity.

SAPPHIRE & ISHMAEL: *(Sing refrain while they join BENJAMIN kneeling at JESUS' feet)* I fall down at Your feet; I fall down at Your feet.
Finally I'm in Your presence.
I fall down at Your feet.

GUARD 1: *(Sings to the tune of "I Surrender All" verse three. Singing to JESUS)* Who are You that we slandered?
Who are You that we killed?
The Holy God incarnate,
Our Messiah has been revealed.

(Sings refrain while falling at JESUS' feet)
I fall down at Your feet; I fall down at Your feet.
Finally I'm in Your presence.
I fall down at Your feet.

NARRATOR: *(To the audience)* Join us as we worship.

JERUSALEM CHOIR: *(Sings refrain)*
I fall down at Your feet; I fall down at Your feet.
Finally I'm in Your presence.
I fall down at Your feet.

(The curtains close.)

A Morning in the Temple

Holy Duties in Herod's Temple

Time: 1 hour

Scene Descriptions & Props*

The Temple Mount

The House of Immersion: The House of Immersion was under the actual Temple. Priests shuttle to and from this place daily to cleanse themselves prior to service in the Temple. Next to the pool is a fire where the Priests warm themselves. White towels are also needed. In Scene 1, the Priests will go to the right side of the audience to the House of Immersion.

Nicanor Gate: The Nicanor Gate is the entry way between the Court of the Women and the Temple Court. The Levitical Choir sings on a platform just inside the Nicanor Gate facing the altar and Sanctuary.

Temple Court: The centerpiece of the Temple Court is the altar, a perfect-square structure which can be ascended and descended with a ramp. Stairs are not permitted. There are three fires on the altar, one of which being a perpetual fire. There is a slaughter area with a table and neat piles of wood in front of the altar close to the audience. To the side of the altar closest to the Sanctuary is the laver (a large basin for ceremonial washing). In this play's scenes, behind the altar is a silver table specifically used to receive the holy vessels. There is also a wall of doorways which depict different chambers. Cast members will only need to enter and exit these chambers to retrieve items. These chambers are the Chamber of Lambs, the Chamber of Vessels, the Place of Fire, the Chamber of Avtinas, and the Chamber of Showbread. During the second scene, the Priests will patrol the Temple Mount and check these chambers. There is also a Chamber of Hewn Stone which needs to be a larger area with a larger opening because many priests enter this area to conduct the selections for each task. During this selection process, a priest must take off his head covering which would be disrespectful in the actual Temple Court.

Chambers in the Temple Court

There were many chambers within the walls of the Temple. Many are not mentioned in the play and do not need to be represented, such as the Chamber of Seals, the Chamber of Wood, the Chamber of the Well, the Chamber of Wardrobes, etc. Several are mentioned and could simply be represented by doorways. Each place is checked by the priests during the morning patrol.

*Sources found in the back of the book.

The Chamber of Lambs: A chamber in which the lambs for sacrifice were kept. It can be depicted by a doorway.

The Place of the Fire: The Place of the Fire was a chamber in the Temple where the priests slept. A fire was kept there. There were stone slabs for the elderly priests to sleep on, and younger priests slept on the floor. The keys to the gates were kept in this chamber so the priests were able to unlock the gates in the morning. The Place of the Fire can be depicted as a doorway.

The Chamber of the Showbread: This is where the showbread was made. The High Priest and his deputy will exit from this chamber with the meal offering. It can be depicted as a doorway.

The Chamber of Wine: This is the location of the libations used in the Temple services. It can be depicted as a doorway.

The Chamber of Musical Instruments: The cymbals, harps, trumpets, and shofar are kept there. It can be depicted by a doorway.

The Chamber of Vessels: There were said to be 93 sacred vessels of silver and gold that were used in the sacred duties of the Temple. The vessels used in this play may be stored on a shelf just inside a doorway. The priests will check these during the morning patrol, and they will retrieve them to put on the silver table of vessels in the Temple Court in Scene 2.

> Scene 1: two gold platters for the High Priest's loaves of the meal offering
> Scene 2: a silver shovel, ashbin, rakes, and forks for use on the altar fire
> Scene 3: a silver shovel, ashbin, rakes, and forks for use on the altar fire
>> a gold cup with which to give the lamb water
>> a gold bowl or basin to catch the lamb's blood
>> a gold bowl to hold the inner organs, a gold bowl to hold the intestines
>> a copper bowl to hold the fine flour
>> two gold platters each holding six of the High Priest's loaves
>> a gold bowl of frankincense and a gold bowl of salt
>> a gold ashbin to hold the ashes for the incense altar
>> a gold receptacle to hold the ash and wicks from the menorah
>> wicks, a gold oil flask, gold tongs, and a brush to remove the wicks and ashes from the menorah

Scene 4: a silver shovel, ashbin, rakes, and forks for use on the altar fire
        a gold bowl to hold the inner organs, a gold bowl to hold the intestines
        a copper bowl to hold the fine flour
        two gold platters each holding six of the High Priest's loaves
        a gold bowl of frankincense and a gold bowl of salt
        a gold ashbin to hold the ashes for the incense altar
        a gold receptacle to hold the ash and wicks from the menorah
        wicks, a gold oil flask, gold tongs, and a brush to remove the wicks and
        ashes from the menorah

The Chamber of Hewn Stone: The Chamber of Hewn Stone is a meeting place for the Priests and is a place of prominence in the play. This is where the priests gather to conduct drawings to determine who will conduct each holy duty. The priests stood in a circle to conduct a drawing. One priest would take off his hat to indicate where the counting started. Since being without a head covering in the Temple Court is considered disrespectful, the drawing was conducted in the chamber.

The Chamber of Avtinas: In this chamber, the Avtinas family made the special incense for the incense altar. Akiva Avtinas will exit the chamber from this doorway to speak to the audience.

The Temple Sanctuary: The Temple proper or Sanctuary consists of three areas: the entrance hall, the Holy Place, and the Holy of Holies (Most Holy Place). There is a door or gate between the entrance hall and the Holy of Holies which must be unlocked every morning and locked every evening. A veil separates the Holy Place and the Holy of Holies (Most Holy Place). This building in our scenes lacks a side wall so the audience can view the interior.

The Entrance Hall: The entrance hall contains features which are noteworthy. On each side of the hall, there are built-in niches where knives are stored. There are also two tables which serve a special purpose in the Temple. A marble table is on the right side of the gate or door which leads to the Holy Place and a gold one on the left. Every Sabbath, 12 freshly-baked loaves of unleavened bread are brought into the Temple to replace those of the previous week on the table of showbread. The freshly baked showbread may be set on the marble table to cool; however, the showbread on the gold table of showbread is considered to have a higher level of sanctity. Once the sacred bread is placed on the gold table of showbread, it can never be "demoted" by being placed on a lesser table, i.e., the marble table. For this reason, the week-old showbread can only be moved to the gold table before being eaten by the priests.

The Holy Place: The Holy Place—the larger area of the Sanctuary—houses the menorah, the table of showbread, and the incense altar. Twelve loaves of unleavened bread and two bowls of frankincense are on the table of showbread, where they would have remained for a week. On the Sabbath, another 12 loaves will be brought in to replace these and sprinkled with the frankincense. The remaining frankincense will remain on the table with the new loaves. The old 12 loaves will be moved to the gold table in the entrance hall and subsequently will be eaten by the Priests. The frankincense that was on the table with the old loaves will be burned on the incense altar before the priests eat the old loaves. The supplies needed for the menorah are a gold oil flask, a gold oil lamp, and a gold receptacle to hold the ashes and spent wicks.

Holy of Holies: Beyond the large veil, the Holy of Holies is empty. In the previous Temple (Solomon's Temple, also called the First Temple), the Holy of Holies held the Ark of the Covenant, but this was either hidden by priests, or stolen or destroyed by the Babylonians when the First Temple was razed in 586 or 587 BC.

Cast Descriptions & Props*

NARRATOR:	The narrator speaks throughout the play. He may be dressed in modern-day clothing, as a priest, or a Levite.
PRIESTS:	The priests are between the ages of 30 and 50. On ordinary days, they wear four white garments: pants, tunics, belts, and hats. First the priests don the pants which are to the knees. The tunic covered the pants. A long belt wraps around the waist and flows down to the ankles. It's debated if the belt is white or (like that of the High Priest) a combination of gold, sky blue, deep red, and crimson. Whichever is used, all priests should be uniform. The belt may be thrown over the left shoulder during their holy tasks so it doesn't

*Sources found in the back of the book.

interfere. The hat is put on last. The priests must always wear a head covering in the since it is considered disrespectful for males to be in the Temple proper without a head covering. They do not wear anything on their feet. All priests will need a torch because duties start pre-dawn. There are a minimum of 16 priests needed in this play.

PRIEST 31 – Chosen to remove the ashes from the altar, dump the water from the laver and refill it, bring new wood and arrange on the fire for offerings. He needs a silver shovel.

PRIEST 1 – One of the eager early-rising priests in Scene 1. He has a speaking part in Scene 2. The person who plays PRIEST 1 may also play one of the priests 18 – 30.

PRIEST 2 – One of the eager early-rising priests in Scene 1. He has a speaking part in Scene 2. The person who plays PRIEST 2 may also play one of the priests 18 – 30.

PRIEST 3 – Chosen to perform the incense offering in the Holy Place in Scene 4. He will need a gold ladle to scoop out the incense During the Priestly Blessing on the steps of the Sanctuary, he will hold the gold ladle.

PRIEST 4 – Chosen to take the offering from midway up the ramp to the fire on the top of the ramp.

PRIEST 18 – Chosen to slaughter the offering. He needs a knife. PRIEST 18 also salts everything that is offered for sacrifice, so he needs a bowl of salt. PRIEST 18 has speaking parts in Scene 4. PRIEST 18 will also be a trumpeter to announce the wine libation in Scene 4, so he will need a fake or real trumpet and sound effects if needed. There is a long blast, two short and then another long blast.

PRIEST 19 – Chosen to dash the blood upon the altar. He needs a gold bowl to catch the blood. PRIEST 19 has a speaking part in Scene 4 also. He will need to carry a torch to help examine the sheep one last time before sacrificing it. He is tasked with giving the sheep water from a gold cup. PRIEST 19 will also be a trumpeter to announce the wine libation in Scene 4, so he will need a fake or real trumpet and sound effects if needed. There is a long blast, two short and then another long blast.

PRIEST 20 – Chosen to remove the ashes from the incense altar. He needs a silver firepan, a gold firepan, and a small brush.

PRIEST 21 – Chosen to attend to the menorah. He needs the gold tongs and brush to remove the spent wicks and ashes, a gold oil flask, a gold receptacle in which the ashes and wicks were placed. The actual menorah was a tall structure, and the priest needed to ascend three stairs to reach the branches. Priest 21 also gives the gate keys of the Temple Sanctuary to give to Ben Gever.

PRIEST 22 – Chosen to carry the head and right back leg of the sacrifice to the altar ramp. He will carry the body parts in his hands. He will need to carry a torch to help examine the sheep one last time before sacrificing it.

PRIEST 23 – Chosen carry the two front legs of the sacrifice to the altar ramp. He will carry the body parts in his hands. He will need to carry a torch to help examine the sheep one last time before sacrificing it.

PRIEST 24 – Chosen to carry the lower spinal column, the tail, and the left back leg of the sacrifice to the altar ramp. He will carry the body parts in his hands. He will need to carry a torch to help examine the sheep one last time before sacrificing it.

PRIEST 25 – Chosen to carry the breast, the throat, and some of the inner organs of the sacrifice to the altar ramp. He needs a gold bowl in which to place the body parts. He will need to carry a torch to help examine the sheep one last time before sacrificing it.

PRIEST 26 – Chosen to carry the two flanks of the sacrifice to the altar ramp. He will carry the body parts in his hands. He will need to carry a torch to help examine the sheep one last time before sacrificing it.

PRIEST 27 – Chosen to carry the intestines of the sacrifice to the altar ramp. He needs a gold bowl in which to place the body parts. He will need to carry a torch to help examine the sheep one last time before sacrificing it.

PRIEST 28 – Chosen to carry the fine flour of the meal offering to the altar ramp. He needs a copper bowl in which to place the flour. He will retrieve the gold bowl of frankincense and sprinkle some on the flour before it is offered.

PRIEST 29 – Chosen to carry the High Priest's meal offering to the altar ramp. The High Priest offers 12 loaves daily, half in the morning and half in the evening sacrifice. So PRIEST 29 needs a gold platter on which to place the six loaves for the morning half of the meal offering. He will sprinkle some frankincense on the six loaves before they are offered.

PRIEST 30 – Chosen to pour the wine libations on the altar. He needs a gold bottle full of a liquid.

GEVINI: Gevini is the Temple Crier or Rooster. He announces the beginning of the day. He may wear priest clothing.

MATYA: Matya is in charge of the drawings to select who performs each task. He instructs the priests to stand in a circle. He is careful never to count the priests but only their fingers. He may wear priest clothing.

HASHABIAH: Hashabiah is Matya's assistant. He takes off a head covering of a random priest to help Matya in choosing priests to conduct the holy duties. He may wear priest clothing.

BEN GEVER: Ben Gever is the gatekeeper. In Scene 3, he also announces that dawn has arrived. It was imperative not to perform the daily sacrifice too early. He may wear priest clothing.

AKIVA AVTINA: The Avtina family was an integral part of the Temple. The Avtinas were the only people who knew the identity of the plant which made the incense rise up in a straight column. Akiva was the head of the clan. He will need a gold incense dish with a piece of linen to cover it. He may wear priest clothing.

HIGH PRIEST: Ananias ben Nedebeus was the High Priest in 50 A.D. On normal days, the High Priest wears eight "gold garments." These consist of the pants, tunic, ephod, robe, belt, breastplate, turban, and gold crown or forehead plate. First the priests don the pants which were to the knees. The tunic covered the pants and is sky blue. It's decorated with bells and pomegranates along the bottom. The ephod is an apron-like piece of gold, sky blue, dark red, and crimson clothing which covers the tunic and robe. There are two sardonyx stones attached to the shoulders of the ephod. The names of the tribes of Israel are engraved on them. The High Priest also wears a square-shaped breastplate of the same colors in a brocade pattern over his heart. It contains four rows of mounted stones with the names of the 12 tribes of Israel. The belt is also gold, sky blue, dark red, and crimson. The High Priest wears a turban head covering of blue or white with a gold crown or forehead plate. He does not wear anything on his feet.

DEPUTY:　　　　The Deputy is a priest who assists the High Priest.

BEN ARZA:　　　Ben Arza is the musician who clanged a cymbal to indicate when the Levites should begin singing their song. He may wear priest clothing.

HUGRAS BEN LEVI:　　　Hugras is the song leader. There is an assigned Psalm for each day which was set to music and sang. Hugras Ben Levi was responsible for leading the correct song daily. He holds a white handkerchief to wave when indicating the beginning of the song. He may wear priest clothing.

LEVITICAL CHOIR:　　　The Levites are adult males. They may wear normal colored robes of townspeople in Biblical times. Their heads must be covered in the Temple at all times. There is a rule that there must be 12 or more adult male Levites in the choir. Children are allowed to participate; however, they don't count toward the 12.

Scene 1
The House of Immersion
Time: 14 minutes

Scenes: Temple Court, Place of the Fire, Chamber of Hewn Stone, House of Immersion
Cast: (19+) NARRATOR; TEMPLE CRIER GEVINI; 13 or more PRIESTS including
PRIEST 1, 2, and 31; SELECTION PRIEST MATYA; MATYA's assistant
HASHABIAH; HIGH PRIEST ANANIAS; the HIGH PRIEST'S DEPUTY
Song: "Whiter than Snow" (with adaptations)
Props: A shofar, white towels for the PRIESTS in the House of Immersion, 12 small
unleavened loaves, 2 gold platters, 1 torch for each PRIEST

(The NARRATOR is standing to the left of the stage. He blows a shofar.)

NARRATOR: We are in Jerusalem, standing on the Temple Mount. It's AD 50,
that is to say *anno Domini*, or the year of our Lord, 50. Jesus died,
was resurrected, and ascended to heaven 20 years ago, and in 20
more years the Romans will come here to this very place and
destroy the Temple, just as Jesus prophesied. Today, while there is
still time, you will have an opportunity to examine the inner
workings of this magnificent edifice and explore the profound
symbolic meaning of the sanctified vessels within these walls.

It's early in the morning, *(PRIESTS 1 and 2 enter from the Place of
the Fire holding torches: one wiping at his eyes and the other
stretching, but both with smiles on their faces.)* even before dawn,
when the zealous priests start to stir from their sleeping quarters in
the Place of the Fire. There's an anticipation in the air. This group
of priests have been waiting for months for their turn to conduct
the Temple duties. The Temple is a hive of activity. The priests
sleep, wash, eat, and serve here for a week at a time. You see,
because the Levites from Aaron's branch of the family tree have
multiplied to such a great number, believed to be more than 7,000

NARRATOR: priests at this time, they have been divided into 24 divisions. Each division serves a week at a time in the Temple. The divisions are further divided into six groups, meaning each group is able to serve one day a week and the Sabbath, wherein the whole division serves. They eagerly await this opportunity because they get to serve only a couple of times a year, with the exception of busy holy days, when all 24 groups are needed.

(The TEMPLE CRIER GEVINI enters holding a torch and stands to the right of the stage. The eager PRIESTS 1 and 2 make their way down to the House of Immersion.)

GEVINI: *(Calling out in a loud voice)* Rise up, priests, to your worship; Levites, to your stands; and Israelites, to your posts.

NARRATOR: *(Motions to GEVINI)* He is the Temple Crier or Rooster. His name is Gevini. It was said that his stentorian voice projected so well, he could be heard in Jericho, which was more than 15 miles away. Gevini was the very Temple Crier on duty when Jesus walked the earth. *(To GEVINI)* Gevini, may we hear your proclamation once again?

GEVINI: Certainly. *(Calling out in a loud voice)* Rise up, priests, to your worship; Levites, to your stands; and Israelites, to your posts.

NARRATOR: He calls out three groups of people, which gives a clear view of the positions held in and around the Temple. The term *Israelites* encompasses the totality of Jews, including women. Some of the Israelites are Levites, who are the descendants of Levi, the third child of Jacob and Rachel. And within the Levite tribe are the priests who are consecrated to do the holy tasks of the Temple. Temple priests must be males from the Levite clan and between 30 and 50 years of age.

(PRIESTS, holding torches, start to enter from the Place of the Fire as if just waking up. They stretch, yawn, and wipe at their eyes.)

NARRATOR: Now I will pass you off to Gevini. He will give you a little history lesson.

GEVINI: *(Notices the audience)* Good morning. I am Gevini. As you can see, I am the Temple crier. I announce the beginning of the day. Welcome to Jerusalem, God's Holy City. *(Stretches his arms out at his sides)* We are on the upper part of Mount Moriah, where the Temple Mount was built. There is exposed bedrock on this site that has come to be known as the Foundation Stone. The wise sages believe the exposed bedrock is the genesis of all creation. The Holy Scriptures say in Isaiah, "So this is what the Sovereign LORD says: 'See, I lay a stone in Zion, a tested stone, a precious cornerstone for a sure foundation. . . .'"

This is the place where Jacob slept and had the encounter with the angel. Hundreds of years later, after King David angered the Lord by ordering a census, a plague killed more than 70,000 men. David repented, and the Lord told him to offer a sacrifice here. During those days, this very spot was used as a threshing floor by Araunah the Jebusite. David paid 600 shekels of gold for the field and an additional 50 shekels of silver for the oxen and the threshing floor. Can you see the symbolism? A threshing floor is the place where the chaff is separated from the wheat, and the Temple of God is where evil is separated from the holy.

Later, David's son Solomon built the First Temple here. The Holy of Holies was built over the Foundation Stone, and that was where the Ark of the Covenant rested. That Temple was destroyed by King Nebuchadnezzar and the Babylonians. Zerubbabel built the Second Temple, and it was remodeled and improved by Herod. The Temple Mount has a long history with the Jewish people and continues to this day to be a place of reverence.

(The remaining PRIESTS, SELECTION PRIEST MATYA, and his assistant, HASHABIAH, enter holding torches and start to line up to go down into the House of Immersion to purify themselves.)

GEVINI: Well, I see the priests are lining up. First things first: they will all go down to the springs to purify themselves by immersion. Even if a priest knows he is ceremonially pure, he must go down to the pools to be purified because of the sanctity of the Temple. No one can enter the Temple, for service or any other reason, without being cleansed. I will take my leave now and join them. *(To the audience)* Enjoy your day at the Holy Temple. *(Joins the line of PRIESTS)*

(They lean their torches against the wall and start to sing "Whiter than Snow" as they each go down one by one and immerse themselves in the water. They come up wiping at their faces—even if there isn't real water.)

PRIESTS: Whiter than snow, yes, whiter than snow,
                       Now wash me, and I shall be whiter than snow.

GEVINI: Oh, how I long to be perfectly whole;
                       I want Thee forever to live in my soul,
                       Break down every idol, cast out every foe;
                       Now wash me and I shall be whiter than snow.

PRIESTS: Whiter than snow, yes, whiter than snow,
                       Now wash me, and I shall be whiter than snow.

GEVINI: Born for your service, it's all that I know
                       To be used for your glory, I'm in Your control.
                       Like a seed being planted, just waiting to grow.
                       Now wash me and I shall be whiter than snow.

PRIESTS: Whiter than snow, yes, whiter than snow,
                       Now wash me, and I shall be whiter than snow.

(The PRIESTS exit with their torches and go to the Place of the Fire to "dry off and change clothes." GEVINI exits. The HIGH PRIEST and his DEPUTY enter. The HIGH PRIEST is holding a torch, and the DEPUTY is holding two gold platters with six loaves of unleavened bread on each.)

NARRATOR: Oh, look, there's the High Priest Ananias ben Nedebeus and his

NARRATOR: deputy. Ananias is already dressed, so he must have already purified himself this morning. He has a reputation of being a violent and greedy man. During the Council of the Sanhedrin, he ordered the Apostle Paul to be struck, and Paul called him a "whitewashed wall." You see, by this time, the appointment as High Priest was no longer a divine installation, but instead more of a political one. I will see if I can get his attention so he will say a few words to you.

(The DEPUTY sets one of the gold platters of six loaves on the table of vessels.)

(Calling to the HIGH PRIEST) High Priest Ananias, excuse me. May we have a moment of your time, please?

(The HIGH PRIEST and DEPUTY approach center stage.)

Sir, please tell us what your deputy has in his hand.

HIGH PRIEST: Good morning. My deputy is carrying my daily meal offering baked into loaves. I offer 12 loaves each day, half in the morning and half *(motions to the loaves remaining on the vessel table)* during the evening sacrifice. They are made of unleavened flour, which symbolizes prayers that are not puffed up, and they are mixed with oil, which represents the spirit of Jehovah. Frankincense will be sprinkled on them which creates a sweet aroma unto the Lord, and they will be offered with praise and thanksgiving.

NARRATOR: We notice that you are dressed differently than the other priests. Can you tell us the difference?

HIGH PRIEST: Yes, the priests *(motions to the DEPUTY)* wear four garments. Deputy, why don't you tell them about the priest's attire.

DEPUTY: We wear a turban head covering, a tunic, pants, and a long belt that we can toss over our left shoulder when we are performing tasks if it gets in the way. It's interesting to note also that when the priestly

73

DEPUTY: garments get too soiled to be cleaned, they are shredded and used as wicks in the menorah and in the large torches in the Court of the Women to light the area during the Festival of Sukkot.

HIGH PRIEST: But the same can't be said of the High Priest's garments. If they are no longer able to be cleaned, they can only be stored away. They can never be thrown away or used for wicks. In addition to the turban head covering, tunic, pants, and belt, I also wear an ephod, a robe, a breastplate, and a gold forehead plate. If you look on my shoulders, *(motions)* you will see there are two sardonyx stones. Those and the stones on the breastplate *(motions)* have the names of the 12 tribes of Israel. According to Jewish tradition, the clothes that we wear in the Temple are considered such an integral part that if we didn't wear them, it would render the service invalid.

DEPUTY: Each garment has a symbolic meaning as well. *(Points to each piece on the HIGH PRIEST as he mentions it)* The tunic is said to atone for killing. The robe covers evil speech. The pants make amends for sexual transgressions. The belt atones for impure thoughts, while the breastplate covers any errors of judgment. The ephod atones for idolatry. The turban compensates for conceit, and the gold crown or forehead plate atones for arrogance.

(The PRIESTS exit the Place of the Fire still holding torches and begin making their way toward the Chamber of Hewn Stone where they lean their torches against the wall again.)

NARRATOR: *(Motions toward the PRIESTS)* It looks like the priests are gathering in the Chamber of Hewn Stone for the first daily selection to determine who will perform which holy tasks.

MATYA: *(Calls out)* Whoever has immersed himself, let him come to draw lots.

HIGH PRIEST: We need to put this on the table.

DEPUTY: Are you offering it today, or will you allow the priests to do it?

HIGH PRIEST: I will allow the priests to do it today.

(The HIGH PRIEST and the DEPUTY walk back toward the table to set the platter down next to the other one and then exit.)

NARRATOR: There are many duties in the Temple. The High Priest may perform any that he chooses or none of them on any given day. It looks like the priests are almost ready to see who will be chosen for the first task of the day. Matya is in charge of doing the selections.

MATYA: Come into the Chamber of Hewn Stone, because one priest must have his head covering removed, and it is not proper to remove it in the Temple. Make a circle around me.

(The PRIESTS make a circle with MATYA on the inside and HASHABIAH on the outside.)

                        We will now select for the first task of the day: removing the ashes from the altar and adding wood for the fire. Priests, please raise one finger, since I must not count people. I will count only your fingers. Please, Hashabiah, my assistant, take off the head covering of one random priest.

(HASHABIAH takes off the hat of one random priest. MATYA speaks quickly so there's no possible way he could have counted to find out the result.)

                        The number is 31. *(MATYA begins to count fingers, starting with the PRIEST whose hat is taken off, and goes around the circle until he lands on 31. That PRIEST is the one chosen to perform the first task.)* You have been chosen to remove the ashes from the altar, dump the water from the laver, and refill it. You will bring new wood, fix the arrangement of wood on the altar, and bring up two smaller pieces of wood to the fire.

(PRIEST 31 nods his head in acceptance. The circle disbands. Each PRIEST grabs his torch and moves to the Temple Court.)

Scene 2
The Dawn Patrol

Time: 10 minutes

Scenes: Temple Court, Temple Chambers

Cast: (17+) NARRATOR; TEMPLE CRIER GEVINI; 13 or more PRIESTS including PRIEST 31, PRIEST 1, and PRIEST 2; SELECTION PRIEST MATYA; his assistant HASHABIAH

Song: "Farther Along" (with adaptations)

Props: 1 torch for each PRIEST conducting the morning patrol, fake fire source, silver altar shovel positioned at the side closest to the Temple Sanctuary, silver ashbin, silver rakes and forks for cleaning the fire, stacks of small logs, burned remains on the fire

NARRATOR: After the first tasks are assigned, the priests line up in two lines to perform the morning patrol around the Temple. Dawn has not broken yet, so they will need torches to light their way. *(The PRIESTS start to slowly retrieve their torches.)* On the Sabbath, the priests do not carry torches. Instead, candles are lit in the Temple court the prior evening. On their patrol, the priests will make sure everything is in order, nothing has happened in the night, and nothing needs special attention before the start of the day. They will check the 93 vessels for use in the Temple duties in the Chamber of Vessels and the animals in the Chamber of the Lambs. They will scan the Chambers of Showbread, Fire, and Seals for any disturbances. But before they perform this task and all subsequent tasks, they bless the Lord.

(The PRIESTS, including PRIEST 31, form two lines.)

PRIESTS: *(With arms raised heavenward)* Blessed are You, Hashem our God, Sovereign of the universe, who has sanctified us in the sanctity of Aaron and commanded us to patrol the Temple at dawn.

PRIESTS:

(They sing to the tune of "Farther Along" as the two lines head to the perpetual fire on the altar to light their torches and then off in opposite directions to circle the Temple. They sing quietly as they walk along moving their torches left and right, looking for any irregularities. They check around the altar, inside the chambers, and all around.)

God, please use me here in this moment.
Lord, You will find me down on my knees.
Take my hands, Lord, make me a servant.
I long to do whatever You please.

(Chorus)
Born in this clan, we're here in God's service,
Working together all the day long;
From sunup to sundown we long for Your presence;
Like incense arising, we'll sing You this song.

My heart's on fire, Lord, come fan the flames.
We're lifting you higher, praising your name.
An altar of brokenness, my past and my wounds.
Just send down your fire, my life to consume.

(Chorus)
Born in this clan, we're here in God's service,
Working together all the day long;
From sunup to sundown we long for Your presence;
Like incense arising, we'll sing You this song.

(The PRIESTS return and meet at the starting point.)

It is well; all is well, and all the vessels are in place.

NARRATOR: All is well! That's what everyone wants to hear.

MATYA: It's as simple as that. This is the fairest way to ensure that each priest has an opportunity to perform a coveted holy duty. There will be three additional selections throughout the day.

77

NARRATOR: Before the chosen priest starts his tasks, the other priests guide him along.

PRIEST 1:   Be careful! Don't forget to wash your hands and feet at the laver before touching anything.

(PRIEST 31 bows in gratitude and starts toward the laver. The other PRIESTS stand together and watch.)

PRIEST 2:   Make sure to use the silver shovel kept in the corner between the western side of the ramp and the southern side of the altar.

PRIEST 31:   Yes, thank you.

NARRATOR: The chosen priest then makes his way to the laver, which was lowered into the water the previous night. A new day means fresh water. A pulley system was devised to lower the laver into a specially made well and raise it again. The pulley system made a very distinct sound. When the priests heard this sound, they shouted out.

PRIESTS: The time has arrived!

NARRATOR: As the priest washes his hands and feet, Gevini will share the history of the laver and the altar.

(PRIEST 31 makes his way to the laver and cleanses his hands and feet while GEVINI speaks.)

GEVINI: The laver is a holy instrument of sanctification. If you remember from the days of the Tabernacle, the righteous women offered their copper mirrors to construct the first laver. Their unselfishness and giving nature has been remembered even unto this day. For this reason, even when everything else was constructed of gold in Solomon's Temple, the laver remained copper. The copper also worked as a mirror and allowed the priests to see themselves. The laver was meant to be a place of introspection and self-judgment.

78

GEVINI: The correct manner in which to wash is to pour water over the right hand and foot first and then the left hand and foot.

(PRIEST 31 leaves the laver and retrieves the silver shovel and ashbin.)

The altar area is said to be the place where God formed Adam from the dust of the ground. You'll remember God told Abraham to go to Mount Moriah and offer his only son, Isaac, as a sacrifice. The altar may be larger now, but this is the very place where, by grace, God provided a ram in the bush and Isaac was spared.

As you can see, the altar is a perfect square. It was constructed of stone and earth. At each of the four corners on top is a horn. These symbolize God's power and salvation in the four corners of the earth. In the book of Exodus, it says that the altar cannot be climbed by steps for the sake of modesty. That is why there is a ramp. Matya will tell you step-by-step what the chosen priest is doing.

(PRIEST 31 walks up the ramp to the altar and stands before the largest fire, which receives the offerings.)

PRIEST 31:   *(Lifts his hands heavenward)* Blessed are You, Hashem our God, Sovereign of the universe, who has sanctified us in the sanctity of Aaron and commanded us to remove the ashes from the altar and add wood to the fire. *(Bends to stir the ashes. He scoops some up.)*

MATYA: As you can see, there are three areas for fires on top of the altar. The largest one is to be used to sacrifice all the offerings. The second one provides the coals for the incense altar within the Sanctuary, and the third is the perpetual fire, which remains lit at all times, as mentioned in Leviticus 6:13: "The fire shall ever be burning upon the altar; it shall never go out."

Now the priest is stirring the coals, and he collects some ashes into the silver coal pan. It's only a small amount, because this task is conducted as a symbolic act of preparing the altar. He carries them down the ramp and places them in a pile called the Place of Ashes.

(PRIEST 31 walks down the ramp carefully with the ashbin and places it on the floor east of the ramp. He returns the shovel to the side of the altar, to be used by PRIEST 21 in Scene 4. The remaining PRIESTS go to the laver to wash their hands and feet.)

MATYA: Now that the chosen priest has completed his task of symbolically removing the ashes, he will retrieve some wood for the fire while the other priests wash their hands and feet at the laver so they can work on the general upkeep of the fires on the altar.

(PRIEST 31 retrieves wood while the other PRIESTS clean up the fires. Some rake and remove debris. Some use the fork to remove burned remains and place them in a pile.)

They take the rakes and large forks and ascend the ramp. They sift through the fire and remove any portions of sacrifices that weren't consumed the day before. They place them in a pile at the side. All these remains are then raked together to the very center of the altar into a pile called "the apple" because of its shape. When "the apple" gets too large, it may be removed to a location outside the city and buried.

(PRIEST 31 ascends the ramp with two pieces of wood and places them on top of the altar. He arranges the wood in neat piles, which will be used as needed on the fires. Some PRIESTS bring more wood and add to the piles.)

As the priests are finishing up, note that the priest chosen for the first task of the day is also adding and arranging wood on the fires. The priests use the flame from the perpetual fire to start the other two fires. Special care is taken to ensure that the choicest branches of the fig tree are used for the second arrangement, which is used to start the fire to burn incense inside the Holy Place. When all of this is conducted, this concludes the tasks for the first daily selection, and all the priests make their way back to the Chamber of Hewn Stone for the second selection of the day.

(PRIEST 31 stays on the altar to watch and stoke the fire.)

Scene 3
The Altar

Time: 16 minutes

Scenes: Temple Court, Chamber of Lambs, Chamber of Vessels, Chamber of Showbread, Chamber of Wine, Chamber of Hewn Stone, Temple Sanctuary

Cast: (20+) NARRATOR; TEMPLE CRIER GEVINI; GATEKEEPER BEN GEVER; 13 or more PRIESTS including PRIESTS 18-30; SELECTION PRIEST MATYA; his assistant HASHABIAH; HIGH PRIEST ANANIAS; the HIGH PRIEST'S DEPUTY

Props: Torches; silver table in the Temple Court to receive the holy vessels (a gold cup to give the lamb water, a gold bowl or basin to receive blood, a gold bowl to hold the inner organs, a gold bowl to hold the intestines, a copper bowl to hold the fine flour, 2 gold platters for the HIGH PRIEST's meal offering loaves, 12 loaves of unleavened bread, a gold ashbin pan, a gold oil flask, gold tongs, a brush, gold oil lamp, a gold receptacle to hold the ash and spent wicks from the menorah, new wicks, a gold bowl of salt, gold bowl of frankincense); a gold wine bottle; knife; 2 keys to open the Temple Sanctuary gates or doors; fake lamb; fake body parts of a lamb (the head, 4 legs, breast, throat, inner organs, 2 flanks, intestines, spinal column and tail); fake blood

(The TEMPLE CRIER GEVINI and the GATEKEEPER BEN GEVER enter and stand by the gate.)

MATYA: Form a circle around me, and we will choose the 13 priests for the second selection of tasks.

(The PRIESTS all gather around again.)

Please hold up a finger. Hashabiah, please remove the head covering of one priest at random. I will choose a number.

(Each PRIEST holds up one finger. HASHABIAH takes off the head covering of one PRIEST. MATYA speaks quickly before he has time to determine who would be chosen.)

MATYA: The number is 18. *(Beginning with the PRIEST with the removed head covering, MATYA counts to 18.)*
You are priest number 18. You will receive the honor of slaughtering the offering. *(Takes a step to the right to the next priest in line, PRIEST 19)* You will receive the honor of dashing the blood upon the altar. *(Takes a step to the right to the next priest in line, PRIEST 20)* You will receive the honor of removing the ashes from the incense altar in the Sanctuary. *(Takes a step to the right to the next priest in line, PRIEST 21)* You will receive the honor of attending to the menorah. *(Takes a step to the right to the next priest in line, PRIEST 22)* You will receive the honor of carrying the head and right back leg of the sacrifice to the altar. *(Takes a step to the right to the next priest in line, PRIEST 23)* You will receive the honor of carrying the two front legs. *(Takes a step to the right to the next priest in line, PRIEST 24)* You will receive the honor of carrying the lower spinal column, the tail, and the left back leg. *(Takes a step to the right to the next priest in line, PRIEST 25)* You will receive the honor of carrying the breast, the throat, and some of the inner organs. *(Takes a step to the right to the next priest in line, PRIEST 26)* You will receive the honor of carrying the two flanks. *(Takes a step to the right to the next priest in line, PRIEST 27)* You will receive the honor of carrying the intestines. *(Takes a step to the right to the next priest in line, PRIEST 28)* You will receive the honor of carrying the fine flour of the meal offering. *(Takes a step to the right to the next priest in line, PRIEST 29)* You will receive the honor of carrying the High Priest's meal offering baked into loaves. *(Takes a step to the right to the next priest in line, PRIEST 30)* And you will receive the honor of pouring the wine libations. That is all for this selection. *(The PRIESTS start moving away to wash at the laver.)* Now, bring a lamb from the Chamber of Lambs for the morning sacrifice.

BEN GEVER: *(Looking out toward the horizon)* The day has dawned!

NARRATOR: Dawn is the first hour of the Jewish day, which is 6:00 a.m., but out of an abundance of caution, the priests wait.

(The PRIESTS depart for their assigned tasks with torches in hand for light, since it is still early in the morning. PRIESTS 20, 21, 28, 29, and 30 go to the Chamber of Vessels and bring out the vessels and place them on a silver table. They need to retrieve a gold cup with which to give the lamb water, a gold bowl or basin to catch the lamb's blood, a gold bowl to hold the inner organs, a gold bowl to hold the intestines, a copper bowl to hold the fine flour, a gold platter holding six of the High Priest's loaves of the meal offering, a gold ashbin to hold the ashes for the incense altar, a gold receptacle to hold the ash and wicks from the menorah, wicks, a gold oil flask, gold tongs, a brush to remove the wicks and ashes from the menorah, a gold bowl of salt, and a gold bowl of frankincense. They leave their torches inside the Chamber of Vessels. PRIESTS 18, 19, 22, 23, 24, 25, 26, and 27 go to the Chamber of Lambs to secure a lamb.)

NARRATOR: The priests, eager to serve in the Temple, must be patient, for if they sacrifice the lamb too early, it will be invalid. So they busy themselves with the holy duties. Some go to the Chamber of Vessels and bring out the holy vessels that will be used during the service, while the priests who won the privilege of sacrificing the lamb go to the Chamber of the Lamb to retrieve the sacrifice. *(PRIESTS 18, 19, 22, 23, 24, 25, 26, and 27 bring out the lamb and look it over with the torch.)* In the Chamber of Lambs, there are always at least six lambs, which have been checked to be free of blemishes. The priests inspect the lamb closely by torchlight one more time before offering it as a sacrifice, for it must be pure just as our God is pure. Only the blood from a pure sacrifice can atone for sins. *(PRIEST 19 retrieves the gold cup from the table of vessels while PRIEST 18 goes to the Temple's entrance hall to retrieve a knife. They meet back at the lamb. PRIEST 19 gives the gives the lamb some water to drink.)* Then they give the lamb a drink of water from the gold cup.

(PRIESTS 20 goes to the table of vessels. PRIEST 20 takes the gold ashbin to hold the ash from the incense altar. PRIEST 21 goes to the Place of the Fire, retrieves the two keys, and gives them to BEN GEVER. PRIEST 21 then approaches the table of vessels to fetch the gold oil lamp to transfer flames, and the gold receptacle to hold the ash from the menorah. PRIEST 28 grabs a copper bowl from the table of vessels and goes to prepare the fine flour from the Chamber of Showbread. PRIEST 30 gathers the remaining torches from the scene and take them with him to the Chamber of Wine to retrieve the gold bottle.

83

He leaves the torches inside.)

NARRATOR: The morning sacrifice cannot be started until the gates of the Temple are opened at the third hour of the Jewish day, which is 9:00 a.m. for us. The priest has already retrieved the keys to the doors or gates and given them to Ben Gever, the Gatekeeper. Ben Gever is responsible for unlocking the gates or doors to the Temple Sanctuary in the morning and locking them at night.

PRIEST 18:   Is it time for slaughter?

(BEN GEVER gazes out toward the horizon.)

BEN GEVER: The sky is illuminated as far as Hebron. *(He unlocks the gate and opens it.)* The gate to the Sanctuary is unlocked.

(PRIESTS 18, 19, 22, 23, 24, 25, 26, and 27 take the lamb to the north of the altar. The PRIESTS tether the sheep to the slaughtering table. PRIEST 18 recites the blessing as PRIEST 27 goes to the table of vessels to retrieve the knife and a gold bowl in which to place the intestines.)

PRIEST 18:   *(Lifts his hands heavenward)* Blessed are You, Hashem our God, Sovereign of the universe, who has sanctified us in the sanctity of Aaron and commanded us to slaughter the sacrificial lamb.

(PRIESTS 18, 19, 22, 23, 24, 25, 26, and 27 make a circle around the lamb to shield the audience from viewing the killing and dismembering of the sheep. PRIESTS 20 and 21 enter the Holy Place.)

NARRATOR: Since they are certain the time has arrived and the gate has been opened, the priests prepare the lamb for slaughter, being careful not to break any bones in the process. As they busy themselves doing that, let's follow along as the other priests enter the Sanctuary, the Holy Place. Here you will see one priest as he cleans out the ashes from the incense altar and the other priest as he improves the light on the menorah. It seems only two of the wicks are still lit from the previous day. When this happens, he

NARRATOR: must first remove all of the burnt wicks and replace them with new wicks and new oil. He will light the other wicks with those that are already burning. If none were found burning, he would kindle them from the perpetual fire on the outer altar.

(PRIEST 20 places the gold basket on the floor between him and the altar.)

PRIEST 20:   *(Lifts his hands heavenward)* Blessed are You, Hashem our God, Sovereign of the universe, who has sanctified us in the sanctity of Aaron and commanded us to remove the ashes from the incense altar. *(He takes handfuls of ashes into his hands and places them in the basket. Then, when just a small amount remains, he sweeps the rest into the basket. He leaves the basket on the floor and leaves the Holy Place when his task is complete.)*

PRIEST 21:   *(Lifts his hands heavenward)* Blessed are You, Hashem our God, Sovereign of the universe, who has sanctified us in the sanctity of Aaron and commanded us to improve the flames on the menorah. *(PRIEST 21 climbs the three stairs to the menorah, uses the gold tongs to remove the burnt wicks of the five westernmost wicks, places them in the gold receptacle and then puts the gold receptacle on the second stair. He pours new oil in the menorah, and adds five new wicks. He leaves the Holy Place when this part of the task is complete. He leaves the gold receptacle and the gold oil flask on the second stair. He will return later to finish the two easternmost flames.)*

PRIEST 18:   The lamb has been slaughtered. Blood was shed to atone for the sins of the people. Each part has been rinsed thoroughly and is ready to be placed on the altar.

(Each PRIEST should be lining up holding the parts of the lamb that he will take to the ramp of the altar. PRIEST 28 enters from the chambers holding a copper bowl of fine flour, and PRIEST 29 retrieves the HIGH PRIEST's six loaves of unleavened bread from the silver vessel table. PRIEST 30 enters with the wine.)

PRIEST 19:   *(Holds up a bowl or basin of lamb's blood)* The lamb's blood was drained into this vessel. I will dash this lamb's blood on the altar. *(Goes to the northeast corner of the altar and lifts the bowl of blood heavenward)* Blessed are You, Hashem our God, Sovereign of the universe, who has sanctified us in the sanctity of Aaron and commanded us to dash the lamb's blood on the altar. *(He sprinkles the blood in a manner such that it will reach the eastern and northern sides of the altar. Next, PRIEST 19 goes to the southwestern corner of the altar and places a second sprinkling in a manner such that the blood will reach the western and southern sides of the altar. The remainder of the blood, he pours at the southern base of the altar, at its southwestern corner.)*

MATYA: Priests, you have the offerings for our Lord. Place them on the ramp.

PRIESTS 22–30:   *(Lift their offerings heavenward and speak in unison)* Blessed are You, Hashem our God, Sovereign of the universe, who has sanctified us in the sanctity of Aaron and commanded us to take our offerings to the ramp of the altar.

(PRIESTS 22 through 30 walk in a line, in the order they were chosen, to the ramp of the altar. They place their offerings on the ramp starting midway up and going down the west side of the ramp, the side closest to the Sanctuary, leaving room for PRIESTS to descend the ramp.)

NARRATOR: Now the offerings must be salted. Leviticus 2:13 says, "With all thine offerings thou shalt offer salt." Salt has many symbolic meanings. It preserves meat, which means that salt is a fitting symbol of eternal duration. It gives food a good flavor. It was long thought to cure some illnesses. In II Kings, Elisha "heals" the poisonous spring near Jericho by throwing salt into it. Salt is a vital nutrient for our bodies. One cannot live without salt.

PRIEST 18:   *(Lifts his hands heavenward)* Blessed are You, Hashem our God, Sovereign of the universe, who has sanctified us in the sanctity of Aaron and commanded us to salt the offerings.

(PRIEST 18 takes some salt from a gold bowl and salts each offering.)

MATYA:	And now it is customary for the priests to go back into the Chamber of Hewn Stone to recite the Ten Commandments, which are in Exodus 20:1–17.

(All the PRIESTS head over to the Chamber of Hewn Stone with MATYA and HASHABIAH. HIGH PRIEST ANANIAS and his DEPUTY reenter. They join the others in the Chamber of Hewn Stone.)

PRIEST 18:	"And God spake all these words, saying, 'I am the LORD thy God, which have brought thee out of the land of Egypt, out of the house of bondage. Thou shalt have no other gods before me."
PRIEST 19:	"Thou shalt not make unto thee any graven image, or any likeness of any thing that is in heaven above, or that is in the earth beneath, or that is in the water under the earth. Thou shalt not bow down thyself to them, nor serve them: for I the LORD thy God am a jealous God, visiting the iniquity of the fathers upon the children unto the third and fourth generation of them that hate me; and shewing mercy unto thousands of them that love me, and keep my commandments."
PRIEST 20:	"Thou shalt not take the name of the LORD thy God in vain; for the LORD will not hold him guiltless that taketh his name in vain."
PRIEST 21:	"Remember the sabbath day, to keep it holy. Six days shalt thou labour, and do all thy work: But the seventh day is the sabbath of the LORD thy God: in it thou shalt not do any work, thou, nor thy son, nor thy daughter, thy manservant, nor thy maidservant, nor thy cattle, nor thy stranger that is within thy gates: For in six days the LORD made heaven and earth, the sea, and all that in them is, and rested the seventh day: wherefore the LORD blessed the sabbath day, and hallowed it."
PRIEST 22:	"Honour thy father and thy mother: that thy days may be long upon the land which the LORD thy God giveth thee."

PRIEST 23:   "Thou shalt not kill."

PRIEST 24:   "Thou shalt not commit adultery."

PRIEST 25:   "Thou shalt not steal."

PRIEST 26:   "Thou shalt not bear false witness against thy neighbour."

PRIEST 27:   "Thou shalt not covet thy neighbour's house, thou shalt not covet thy neighbour's wife, nor his manservant, nor his maidservant, nor his ox, nor his ass, nor any thing that is thy neighbour's."

MATYA: Then they recite the Shema, which is a compilation of several Scriptures, one of which is Deuteronomy 6:4–9.

HIGH PRIEST: "Hear, O Israel: The LORD our God is one LORD."

PRIESTS: "Blessed be the Name of His glorious kingdom for ever and ever."

HIGH PRIEST: "And thou shalt love the LORD thy God with all thine heart, and with all thy soul, and with all thy might. And these words, which I command thee this day, shall be in thine heart: And thou shalt teach them diligently unto thy children, and shalt talk of them when thou sittest in thine house, and when thou walkest by the way, and when thou liest down, and when thou risest up. And thou shalt bind them for a sign upon thine hand, and they shall be as frontlets between thine eyes. And thou shalt write them upon the posts of thy house, and on thy gates."

MATYA: Deuteronomy 1:13–21.

HIGH PRIEST: *(The PRIESTS may join in if they wish.)* "And it shall come to pass, if ye shall hearken diligently unto my commandments which I command you this day, to love the LORD your God, and to serve him with all your heart and with all your soul, that I will give you the rain of your land in his due season, the first rain and the latter rain, that thou mayest gather in thy corn, and thy wine, and thine

HIGH PRIEST: oil. And I will send grass in thy fields for thy cattle, that thou mayest eat and be full. Take heed to yourselves, that your heart be not deceived, and ye turn aside, and serve other gods, and worship them; and then the LORD's wrath be kindled against you, and he shut up the heaven, that there be no rain, and that the land yield not her fruit; and lest ye perish quickly from off the good land which the LORD giveth you. Therefore shall ye lay up these my words in your heart and in your soul, and bind them for a sign upon your hand, that they may be as frontlets between your eyes. And ye shall teach them your children, speaking of them when thou sittest in thine house, and when thou walkest by the way, when thou liest down, and when thou risest up. And thou shalt write them upon the door posts of thine house, and upon thy gates: That your days may be multiplied, and the days of your children, in the land which the LORD sware unto your fathers to give them, as the days of heaven upon the earth."

MATYA: And finally, Numbers 15:37–41 says,

PRIESTS: "And the Lord spake unto Moses, saying, Speak unto the children of Israel, and bid them that they make them fringes in the borders of their garments throughout their generations, and that they put upon the fringe of the borders a ribband of blue: And it shall be unto you for a fringe, that ye may look upon it, and remember all the commandments of the LORD, and do them; and that ye seek not after your own heart and your own eyes, after which ye use to go a whoring: That ye may remember, and do all my commandments, and be holy unto your God. I am the LORD your God, which brought you out of the land of Egypt, to be your God: I am the LORD your God."

MATYA: And that concludes the morning recitation of the Ten Commandments and the Shema.

Scene 4
The Holy Place
Time: 20 minutes

Scenes: Temple Court, Sanctuary, Chamber of Hewn Stone, Chamber of Avtinas, Nicanor Gate

Cast: (38+) NARRATOR; TEMPLE CRIER GEVINI; 16 or more PRIESTS including PRIESTS 3, 4, and 18–31; SELECTION PRIEST MATYA; his assistant HASHABIAH; AKIVA AVTINAS; HIGH PRIEST; HIGH PRIEST's DEPUTY; CYMBAL PLAYER BEN ARZA; SONG LEADER HUGRAS BEN LEVI; 12 or more LEVITES in the LEVITICAL CHOIR including LEVITE 1, LEVITE 2, LEVITE 3

Song: "In the Sweet By and By" (with adaptations)

Props: Altar rakes, shovels; vessels (gold incense dish with lid, a gold ladle, a gold fire pan, a silver fire pan, a gold oil flask, a gold receptacle for the spent wicks and ashes from the menorah, a gold bowl to hold the inner organs, a gold bowl to hold the intestines, a copper bowl to hold the fine flour, 2 gold platter for the HIGH PRIEST's loaves, a gold bowl of salt, gold bowl of frankincense); a gold wine bottle, fake body parts of a lamb (the head, 4 legs, breast, throat, inner organs, 2 flanks, intestines, spinal column and tail); handkerchief for HUGRAS BEN LEVI, 2 silver trumpets for PRIESTS 18 and 19; cymbals, trumpets, and harps for the LEVITES

MATYA:	Attention. It's time for the next selection, but only priests who have never offered incense may join.
PRIEST 18:	I have never.
PRIEST 19:	Nor I.

(PRIESTS 3, 4, 22, 23, 24, 25, 26, and 27 each raise a finger showing they also haven't. While the NARRATOR is talking, MATYA, HASHABIAH, and PRIESTS 18, 19, 22, 23, 24, 25, 26, and 27 enter the Chamber of Hewn Stone, leaving the other PRIESTS to work tending to the fires on the altar.)

NARRATOR: As the priests make their way to the Chamber of Hewn Stone for the selection of who will offer the incense in the Holy Place, I will give you a background of this most beloved and coveted duty in the Temple. Tradition says the Creator so loved the incense that He rewarded the giver with blessings from heaven of prosperity and safety, as it states in Deuteronomy 33:10–11: "They shall teach Jacob thy judgments, and Israel thy law: they shall put incense before thee, and whole burnt sacrifice upon thine altar. Bless, LORD, his substance, and accept the work of his hands; smite through the loins of them that rise against him, and of them that hate him, that they rise not again."

(As in the previous selections, they silently make a circle around MATYA, and HASHABIAH takes off the head covering of one PRIEST. Each of the PRIESTS holds up one finger, and MATYA silently counts by pointing at each finger, going around the circle a couple of times until he finally puts his hand on the shoulder of PRIEST 3.)

Because of this, it is a once-in-a-lifetime opportunity. The Talmud states that in all of the hundred years of the Temple's existence, no priest ever repeated the incense service. This just shows the number of priests in service, which was said to be over 7,000 in this time period. It also explains why they were so zealous to be a part of any small task in the Temple.

MATYA: *(To PRIEST 3)* You are chosen to offer incense to God!

PRIEST 3:   *(Raises his hands to heaven)* Thank you, God of heaven, for the chance to work in Your Holy Temple. I am humbled by the opportunity.

MATYA: Now, go wash and attend to your duties. *(Steps back out into the altar area and speaks to all the PRIESTS)* Come for the final selection: We will choose a priest to take the offerings up from the ramp to the fire so the sacrifice may be burned unto the Lord.

(PRIEST 3 goes to the laver and washes his hands and feet. PRIESTS 20 and 21 join him at the laver because they will have to go back in to the Holy Place to finish their duties. They wash their hands and feet as well.)

NARRATOR: As MATYA is doing the selection of the priests who will take the offering to the fire to be burned, let's take notice of Akiva Avtinas as he brings the incense.

(AKIVA AVTINAS exits the Chamber of Avtinas holding a gold basket of incense with a lid. He talks as the PRIESTS continue to wash at the laver.)

AKIVA AVTINAS: *(To the audience)* I am Akiva of the Avtinas family. My family and I work here in the Chamber of Avtinas. We were appointed by the Sanhedrin to produce the incense for the Temple. Exodus 30:34–36 says, "And the LORD said unto Moses, Take unto thee sweet spices, stacte, and onycha, and galbanum; these sweet spices with pure frankincense: of each shall there be a like weight: And thou shalt make it a perfume, a confection after the art of the apothecary, tempered together, pure and holy: And thou shalt beat some of it very small, and put of it before the testimony in the tabernacle of the congregation, where I will meet with thee: it shall be unto you most holy." These verses mention only five of the 11 ingredients in the incense. Many of the herbs and spices are rare, and some can be obtained only in exotic and distant lands. It's a closely guarded secret. As a matter of fact, the identity of the herb ma'aleh ashan, which causes the smoke to rise up in a straight column, is known only to my family. We do not want this information to get into the wrong hands. This incense is only for the One True Living God. Amen.

(The other PRIESTS— 4, 18, 19, 22, 23, 24, 25, 26, and 27—go to the Chamber of Hewn Stone for the last selection. While the NARRATOR is talking, MATYA and HASHABIAH conduct the selection quickly. As in the previous selections, the PRIESTS silently make a circle around MATYA, and HASHABIAH takes off the head covering of one PRIEST. Each of the PRIESTS holds up one finger, and MATYA silently counts by pointing at each finger, going around the circle a couple of times until he finally puts his hand on the shoulder of PRIEST 4. PRIEST 4 and the other PRIESTS go to wash at the laver. PRIEST 3 goes over to the table with the vessels and retrieves the gold ladle for the incense.)

AKIVA AVTINAS: *(To PRIEST 3)* I have the special incense ready here. Half of the incense will be burned during the morning, and you'll offer the

AKIVA AVTINAS: other half in the evening.

(PRIEST 3 dips the ladle into the gold incense dish and takes out a scoopful. AKIVA AVTINAS covers the dish with the lid and continues to hold it until it's time for him to take his place outside the Sanctuary to offer a blessing. He may participate in the singing and worship in the Temple Court as he waits. PRIEST 20 has already cleaned the ashes from the incense altar. Now he goes over to the table to retrieve the silver fire pan and the gold fire pan. PRIEST 21 also readies himself to join them, so he can finish his duties with the menorah.)

NARRATOR: Notice the priest has a gold fire pan and a silver fire pan. This is to distinguish the holy from the common. The priest will use the silver fire pan in the Temple Court . . .

(PRIEST 20 sets the gold fire pan at the bottom of the ramp. He carries the silver fire pan with him up the ramp to the altar and scoops up coals with it from the perpetual fire. He comes back down and pours the coals into the gold fire pan.)

and the gold fire pan in the Holy Place. Only gold vessels may be used in the Sanctuary.

(PRIESTS 3 and 21 join PRIEST 20 as he walks toward the Holy Place. PRIEST 21 reaches down and picks up, from its place leaning against the altar, the shovel that was used by PRIEST 31 to remove the ashes. PRIEST 21 throws the shovel against the side of the altar, and it makes a loud, jarring sound, which prompts everyone to scramble for their positions. The LEVITICAL CHOIR starts to form on the platform just inside the Nicanor Gate. Some are carrying instruments such as cymbals, trumpets, and harps. The HIGH PRIEST and his DEPUTY wash their hands and feet, then go into the Holy Place, where they prostrate themselves as the incense is being lit.)

Did you hear that sound? The sound of the shovel crashing against the side of the altar? You may think it was a result of carelessness, but it wasn't. The sound of the shovel hitting the side of the altar is actually a signal to all in the Temple Courtyard. It tells everyone that several things are about to take place in the Holy Place: First, three priests are entering the Holy Place. One is going to finish improving the remaining wicks on the menorah. The second priest

93

NARRATOR: is putting the hot coals on the incense altar, and the third is going to burn the incense. The sound was also a signal for the Levites in the Temple Courtyard to assemble on the platform for the daily song that was sung while the wine was being poured out on the altar. Let's watch as the chosen priest takes the offering up to be sacrificed. It looks like the High Priest is laying his hands on the offering in prayer, asking God to accept the sacrifice.

(The PRIESTS have finished washing at the laver. The HIGH PRIEST and his DEPUTY exit the Holy Place and go up to the top of the ramp. PRIEST 28 retrieves the bowl of frankincense from the table of vessels. PRIESTS 22, 23, 24, 25, 26, 27, 28, 29, and 30 line up to hand their parts of the offering to PRIEST 4. PRIEST 22 ascends halfway, retrieves the head and back leg, hands them to PRIEST 4, and walks down and away from the altar. The HIGH PRIEST puts his hand on the offering as if blessing it.)

PRIEST 19:   *(Lifts the head and back leg heavenward)* Blessed are You, Hashem our God, Sovereign of the universe, who has sanctified us in the sanctity of Aaron and commanded us to burn the sacrifice with fire. *(Throws the pieces into the fire.)*

(PRIEST 23 ascends halfway, retrieves the two front legs, hands them to PRIEST 4, and walks down and away from the altar. The HIGH PRIEST puts his hand on the offering, then PRIEST 4 throws it into the fire. PRIEST 24 ascends halfway, retrieves the lower spinal column, the tail, and the left back leg, hands them to PRIEST 4, and walks down and away from the altar. The HIGH PRIEST puts his hand on the offering, then PRIEST 4 throws it into the fire. PRIEST 25 ascends halfway, retrieves the breast, the throat, and some of the inner organs, hands them to PRIEST 4, and walks down and away from the altar. The HIGH PRIEST puts his hand on the offering, then PRIEST 4 throws it into the fire. PRIEST 26 ascends halfway, retrieves the two flanks, hands them to PRIEST 4, and walks down and away from the altar. The HIGH PRIEST puts his hand on the offering, then PRIEST 4 throws it into the fire. PRIEST 27 ascends halfway, retrieves the bowl of intestine, hands it to PRIEST 4, and walks down and away from the altar. The HIGH PRIEST puts his hand on the offering, then PRIEST 4 throws it into the fire. PRIEST 28 ascends halfway, sprinkles frankincense on the bowl of fine flour, before picking it up and handing it to PRIEST 4. PRIEST 28 walks down and away from the altar. He hands the bowl of frankincense to PRIEST 29. The HIGH PRIEST puts his hand on the offering, then PRIEST 4 pours the flour into the fire. PRIEST 29 ascends and sprinkles the platter

94

of six of the HIGH PRIEST's meal-offering loaves with frankincense, hands it to PRIEST 4, and walks down, and away from the altar. He returns the gold bowl of frankincense to the table of vessels. The HIGH PRIEST puts his hand on the offering, then PRIEST 4 throws it into the fire. The NARRATOR speaks as HUGRAS BEN LEVI ascends the ramp. All the PRIESTS who finished their part of handing off the sacrifice can go to the laver and wash their hands and feet. Then they busy themselves until the singing starts. When the singing starts, they may worship and sing as well.)

NARRATOR: We are watching the High Priest's daily meal offering being taken up the ramp. Notice as the priest sprinkles the meal offering loaves with frankincense just as the High Priest mentioned earlier. Hugras ben Levi, the song leader, is following behind. Let's listen in.

(While PRIEST 4 offers the HIGH PRIEST's meal offering—six loaves—HUGRAS BEN LEVI stands on one of the rams (or corners) of the altar. There is a bustle of activity going on in the Temple Courtyard and the Holy Place. Everyone is making sure to get to their area and start their tasks. The LEVITICAL CHOIR is ready and eagerly waiting. PRIEST 30 is preparing to go up the altar ramp with the wine libation, which will be poured out during the song.)

PRIEST 30:   *(Lifts the wine bottle heavenward)* Blessed are You, Hashem our God, Sovereign of the universe, who has sanctified us in the sanctity of Aaron and commanded us to pour out the libation on the altar during the singing of the psalm. *(Waits for the singing to start before pouring the wine)*

(The HIGH PRIEST and the DEPUTY leave the altar and go to wash at the laver. PRIESTS 20, 21, and 23 make their way back to the Holy Place. The HIGH PRIEST and the DEPUTY enter the Holy Place also and wait for the incense to be lit. BEN ARZA is standing by the table for the vessels. PRIESTS 18 and 19 stand on either side of BEN ARZA with two silver trumpets in their hands. They sound a long blast, two short, and then another long blast as HUGRAS BEN LEVI ascends the ramp to the altar along with PRIEST 30, who is holding the wine libation.)

HUGRAS   This is a special time in the Temple. Each day of the week a
BEN LEVI: different psalm is sung. Today being the first day of the week, we

HUGRAS
BEN LEVI: will sing Psalm 24, which says, "The earth is the LORD's, and the fulness thereof; the world, and they that dwell therein."

(BEN ARZA clangs the cymbals together to announce the beginning of the song. HUGRAS BEN LEVI raises his handkerchief to indicate the beginning of the singing. The LEVITICAL CHOIR sings to the tune of "In the Sweet By and By." During the first stanza and chorus, PRIEST 21 attends to the menorah, relighting the other two wicks that weren't improved earlier. He then prostrates himself toward the Holy of Holies, rises, takes the gold oil flask from the second step, and comes out. He stands outside the Sanctuary holding the gold oil flask in his hands while he waits for the end of the psalm to join in with the Priestly Blessing. PRIEST 20 smooths out the coals on the incense altar with the back of the gold fire pan. He prostrates himself, rises, and comes out, joining PRIEST 21. PRIEST 20 holds the gold fire pan as he waits to join in with the Priestly Blessing. PRIEST 3 lights the incense, and the smoke goes up in a straight column. The HIGH PRIEST and his DEPUTY prostrate themselves toward the Holy of Holies. This is a signal to all the other PRIESTS to enter the Holy Place and prostrate themselves toward the Holy of Holies. All the PRIESTS will eventually come and prostrate themselves in the Holy Place before the end of the song. Then they leave and either go back to the Temple Court to worship or stand outside the Sanctuary waiting for the priestly blessing.)

LEVITES: *(Sing to the tune of "In the Sweet By and By")*
The earth's the Lord's, and all that dwell therein.
He formed it upon the mighty seas.
Who shall ascend to this blessed holy place?
Oh dear Lord, we long to see your face.

(Chorus)
Oh, who *is* this King?
The Lord of hosts so strong and mighty.
Oh, who *is* this King?
Fierce in battle, our God almighty.

(The music continues to play. PRIESTS 18 and 19 sound another long blast with the trumpets. Everyone prostrates himself except PRIESTS 18 and 19, BEN ARZA, and others who have specific tasks.)

LEVITE 1:   "The earth is the LORD's, and the fulness thereof; the world, and they that dwell therein. For he hath founded it upon the seas, and established it upon the floods. Who shall ascend into the hill of the LORD? or who shall stand in his holy place? He that hath clean hands, and a pure heart; who hath not lifted up his soul unto vanity, nor sworn deceitfully."

(Everyone stands back up for the next stanza and chorus. During this, PRIEST 3 prostrates himself and then rises and exits with the gold ladle and lid. He stands outside the Sanctuary along with PRIESTS 20 and 21. At the same time, PRIEST 30 pours out the wine libation onto the fire. When he is finished, he goes inside the Holy Place and prostrates himself toward the Holy of Holies before joining PRIESTS 20, 21, and 23 outside the Sanctuary.)

LEVITES: *(Continuing to sing to the tune of "In the Sweet By and By")*
He'll receive the blessing from the Lord
And righteousness from God up above.
This generation is seeking your face,
Sending up incense full of our love.

(Chorus)
Oh, who *is* this King?
The Lord of hosts so strong and mighty.
Oh, who *is* this King?
Fierce in battle, our God almighty.

(The music continues to play. PRIESTS 18 and 19 sound a long blast with the trumpets. Everyone prostrates himself except PRIESTS 18 and 19, BEN ARZA, and others who have specific tasks. Any remaining PRIESTS may enter the Holy Place to prostrate themselves toward the Holy of Holies. AKIVA AVTINAS brings the gold incense dish and joins the PRIESTS outside the Sanctuary. During the third stanza and chorus, everyone starts to assemble on the steps outside. They all sing and worship together with hands raised during the last stanza and chorus.)

LEVITE 2:   "He shall receive the blessing from the LORD, and righteousness from the God of his salvation. This is the generation of them that seek him, that seek thy face, O Jacob. Selah."

(Everyone stands back up for the next verse.)

LEVITES: *(Continuing to sing to the tune of "In the Sweet By and By")*
                          Lift up your heads, gates be lifted up,
                          Ye everlasting doors open wide
                          And the King of glory shall come in
                          In my heart you're welcome to reside.

                          (Chorus)
                          Oh, who *is* this King?
                          The Lord of hosts so strong and mighty.
                          Oh, who *is* this King?
                          Fierce in battle, our God almighty.

(The music continues to play. PRIESTS 18 and 19 sound a long blast with the trumpets. Everyone prostrates himself except PRIESTS 18 and 19, BEN ARZA, and others who have specific tasks.)

LEVITE 3:   "Lift up your heads, O ye gates; and be ye lift up, ye everlasting
                          doors; and the King of glory shall come in. Who is this King of
                          glory? The LORD strong and mighty, the LORD mighty in battle.
                          Lift up your heads, O ye gates; even lift them up, ye everlasting
                          doors; and the King of glory shall come in. Who is this King of
                          glory? The LORD of hosts, he is the King of glory. Selah."

(PRIEST 31 joins the other PRIESTS outside the Sanctuary. He is holding the gold ashbin. The HIGH PRIEST and his DEPUTY join them as well.)

(After the PRIESTS emerge from the Sanctuary, whether after prostrating themselves or after conducting their assigned duties, they stand on the stairs outside the Holy Place facing the altar and the LEVITICAL CHOIR. The five PRIESTS holding sacred vessels stand in a row: PRIEST 31 with the gold ashbin, PRIEST 20 with the gold fire pan for the incense coals, PRIEST 21 with the gold oil flask, PRIEST 3 with the gold ladle that held incense, and AKIVA AVTINAS with the gold incense bowl. The PRIESTS not holding sacred objects stand behind them in another row on a raised surface. The HIGH PRIEST and his DEPUTY are in the center of the top row. The PRIESTS on the top row along with the HIGH PRIEST'S DEPUTY lift their hands to make the sign of the letter shin, as

shown in the illustration below, at the height of their shoulders, while the HIGH PRIEST only raises his hands up to his breastplate or his chest.)

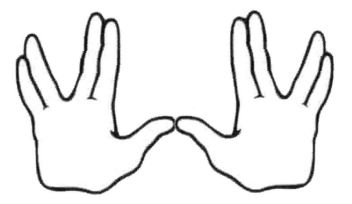

NARRATOR: And now the priests are preparing to give the Priestly Blessing, which beseeches God to accept and find the sacrifice pleasing. Its purpose is also to bless the congregation, as is discussed in Leviticus 9:22, where it says, "And Aaron lifted up his hand toward the people, and blessed them." Notice the priests have their hands raised above their heads, with their hands forming the Hebrew letter sign of *shin*, which also stands for the Hebrew name of God: *Shaddai*. The Priestly Blessing can be found in Numbers 6:24–26.

PRIESTS &
HIGH PRIEST: "The LORD bless thee, and keep thee."

LEVITES: Amen.

PRIESTS &
HIGH PRIEST: "The LORD make his face shine upon thee, and be gracious unto thee."

LEVITES: Amen.

PRIESTS &
HIGH PRIEST: "The LORD lift up his countenance upon thee, and give thee peace."

LEVITES: Blessed are You, Lord God of Israel, from everlasting to everlasting. Amen.

NARRATOR: There are two sacrifices every day. This marks the end of the morning sacrifice. In God's perfect plan, the timeline of the daily sacrifices aligned with the crucifixion of Jesus Christ. As you saw, the first lamb is brought out and tied to the altar at the first hour, which is our 6:00 a.m. This was the same time that Jesus was brought before Pilate. The first lamb was sacrificed at the third hour, which is 9:00 a.m. Jesus was nailed to the cross at that same time. The second lamb of the day is brought out at the sixth hour of the day. That's when Jesus cried out, "My God, my God, why hast Thou forsaken me?" During the ninth hour, or 3:00 p.m., the second lamb is sacrificed. This was the exact time that Jesus breathed his last breath and the veil was torn. So you can see how Jesus Christ fulfilled the law of the sacrifice. He encompassed the sacred. I don't know about you, but that's enough to make me want to worship the King of Kings and Lord of Lords.

PART TWO

MODERN BIBLE CHARACTERS

Modern-Day Jonah

Topic: Your Sin Affects Many
Use: Skit or Puppet Show
Cast: (10+) JONAH, GOD (a disembodied voice), AMITTAI (a disembodied voice on the phone), MAN 1, SAILOR 1, SAILOR 2, MORE SAILORS, SHIP's CAPTAIN, GREAT FISH
Props: A cellphone, selfie stick, notification sounds, ringing sound, shirts, backpack, pier, 2 ships, NINEVEH sign, TARSHISH sign, pebbles or sticks to cast lots, boxes (cargo)
Time: 12 minutes

(JONAH wakes up and pulls out his phone.)

JONAH:	Time for my morning devotions. Let me find the Scripture app on my phone here. *(Scrolls through his phone)* Genesis, Exodus, Leviticus . . . Oh yes, I love this verse: "For thou *art* an holy people unto the LORD thy God, and the LORD hath chosen thee to be a peculiar people unto himself, above all the nations that *are* upon the earth." *Lifts his hand in praise)* Yes, Lord, I receive it.
GOD:	Jonah.

(JONAH keeps his hand in the air and turns his head to the sound of the voice.)

JONAH:	*(With wide eyes)* Yes? Is that You, God?
GOD:	Yes, Jonah, arise, go to Nineveh, that great city.
JONAH:	Nineveh? *(Puts his hand down and starts to scroll on his phone again)* Have you seen what those people are up to over there in Nineveh? Look. *(Holds his phone up toward heaven as if trying to let GOD see)* I joined the People of Nineveh group on InstaTwitFace and they are doing the craziest things over there.

GOD: Yes, I know, Jonah. I know everything. I'm God. Go to Nineveh and cry against it; for their wickedness is come up before Me.

JONAH: Wouldn't my time be better spent making preaching videos? You know, creating content for my platform? I want to be an influencer . . . for You, of course.

GOD: Jonah, just go to Nineveh like I asked. I will be watching. Have a nice day.

(JONAH shakes his head, stands up, and takes a few selfies.)

JONAH: *(Talking to himself)* He wants me to go to Nineveh? Those people are so evil; they'll probably kill me for telling them to turn from their wicked ways.

(A notification sounds on the phone. JONAH looks at it.)

               Well, would you look at that! I just got an event notification from the Joppa Cruise Line. Seems they are taking a trip to Tarshish. That would be much better than Nineveh. Let me call someone.

(JONAH dials the phone. AMITTAI answers. He is not onstage.)

AMITTAI: Hello.

JONAH: Hi, Dad, it's Jonah.

AMITTAI: Well, hello, Son, how are you on this wonderful day?

JONAH: Pretty good. I was just wondering if you could CashApp me a few gold coins.

AMITTAI: A few gold coins. Why? What's going on?

JONAH: I just wanted to take a little trip over to Tarshish. Just a little getaway for a while.

AMITTAI:	And you want me to finance your trip?
JONAH:	Well, I'll pay you back.
AMITTAI:	Let me ask you a question, Jonah. What is my profession?
JONAH:	You're a prophet, Dad.
AMITTAI:	Exactly. And what is it about prophets that is unlike other people?
JONAH:	They know things . . . *(pauses)* Oh.
AMITTAI:	Yes, so I don't think I can help you with your trip to Tarshish. Maybe you should reconsider and head on over to Nineveh.
JONAH:	*(Defeated)* I'll talk to you later, Dad.
AMITTAI:	I can't wait to hear the good report from Nineveh. Bye-bye.

(JONAH puts a few shirts in a backpack and throws it on his back. He heads off to the pier. He stands between the two ships. MAN 1 and SAILOR 1 are holding signs, one saying Nineveh and the other Tarshish. JONAH turns around and starts to take selfies holding up the peace sign and making duck lips in front of the two boats.)

MAN 1:	*(Points)* Take a trip to Nineveh. Nice scenic views. Great night life.
SAILOR 1:	*(Points to the ship)* Take a trip to Tarshish. Wonderful food and a fun time.
JONAH:	Let me post my selfie first. *(Presses keys on the phone and talks as he is typing in the words)* Hashtag: Living my best life. *(Looks up)* Hope my pastor doesn't see that. *(Nervously laughs, then asks the audience)* OK, where should I go? Should I go to Tarshish, or should I go to Nineveh like God told me? *(Waits for audience to answer, then crosses his arms in displeasure when the audience*

| JONAH: | *says Nineveh)* Tarshish it is! *(If the audience reacts)* I'm going to block every one of you on my InstaTwitFace. I don't need this kind of negativity in my life. |

| CAPTAIN: | All aboard. |

(JONAH and SAILOR 1 get on the ship, where the CAPTAIN, SAILOR 2, and other SAILORS are already aboard.)

| JONAH: | OK, I think I'm going to go live. *(Puts his phone on a selfie stick and holds it up as if recording)* Hello, everyone, I am going live here on this beautiful ship heading toward Tarshish. I hear it's a nice little town. If we look this way, you'll see the captain. *(Holds camera toward the CAPTAIN)* Say hello, Captain. *(The CAPTAIN holds his hand up in front of the camera as if he's shy.)* Some folks are scared of the camera, I suppose. *(Pans in the opposite direction, where a dark cloud is forming)* And if we look this way, we can see the great expanse of the sea and . . . oh my, look at that cloud, everyone. *(Looks closely at his phone)* Oh no, I lost signal. The WiFi is terrible out here on the Mediterranean Sea. If there's no WiFi, I might as well take a nap. |

(The wind starts to blow. The ship starts to rock. The CAPTAIN and the other people onboard start to exaggerate being tossed to and fro while JONAH sleeps undisturbed.)

| SAILOR 2: | Baal, help me! We are going to die. |

| SAILOR 1: | Baal, can you hear us? You are the god of the heavens and the seas. |

| SAILOR 2: | Baal must be sleeping like Jonah. Let's throw over some cargo to lighten the ship. |

| SAILOR 1: | Good idea! |

(The SAILORS throw over a few boxes. Everyone continues to be tossed to and fro with the ship. The CAPTAIN approaches JONAH.)

CAPTAIN:	*(Grabs JONAH and shakes him)* How can you sleep? Get up and call upon your God. Their god is useless; maybe your God can help.

(JONAH wakes up, stretches, and is shocked to see the storm. He holds on to the side of the ship.)

SAILOR 2:	If the gods are going to let us all die, someone on this ship must've done something really bad. Come! Let's cast lots to find out who is responsible for this calamity.

(SAILOR 2 casts lots. Then everyone on the boat turns at the same time to stare at JONAH. JONAH laughs nervously.)

JONAH:	What happened was . . . I was minding my own business when God, my God—you know, the One who made the heavens, the sea, and the dry land—He told me to go to Nineveh. I just happened to decide to disobey Him and go with you guys to Tarshish instead.
CAPTAIN:	*(In anger)* You did what?!
JONAH:	What happened was . . .
CAPTAIN:	*(Yells)* I heard you the first time! Your disobedience is going to get all of us killed.
JONAH:	Look, I didn't mean to cause you problems.

(The CAPTAIN comes toward JONAH with a sword. JONAH jumps into the arms of one of the SAILORS if possible.)

JONAH:	Why don't you just toss me overboard?
SAILOR 2:	My pleasure.
JONAH:	*(As he is falling into the sea)* Will you call my dad when you get a signal?

(The GREAT FISH comes and swallows JONAH whole. The voice of GOD is heard.)

GOD: I'll let you stay in the belly of the Great Fish for three days and see if you are ready to obey.

(JONAH takes out his phone.)

JONAH: I can't believe I have service here. *(Dials frantically on his phone)* 911. Yes, 911? I need help. Can you send someone to help me? *(Pauses)* Where am I? *(Pauses)* Well, that's the funny thing. *(Laughs nervously)* See, I just happen to be in the belly of a great big fish. *(Pauses)* Yes, in the middle of the Mediterranean Sea. No, this is not a prank call. Hello? Hello? *(In frustration and distress, JONAH sits down and covers his face.)* I have really messed everything up. *(With hands upraised)* In my distress I called to the Lord, and He answered me. From the belly of death I called for help, and You heard my voice. For You cast me into the deep, into the heart of the seas, and the current swirled about me. Please forgive me, Lord. I know I have sinned. I disobeyed You. If You will give me another chance, I will fulfill what I have vowed.

GOD: OK, Great Fish, it has been three days. You can spit Jonah out onto dry land.

FISH: My pleasure.

(JONAH is expelled from the GREAT FISH. He falls on his face on the beach.)

GOD: Jonah, get up! Go to the great city of Nineveh and proclaim the message that I give you.

JONAH: Yes, Lord, I will go anywhere You say. I'm so sorry for disobeying You. I almost caused the death of the people on the ship. My actions hurt so many people. *(Waves at the audience)* I'll see you guys later. I have to go to Nineveh.

(JONAH exits.)

Modern-Day Lot's Wife

Topic: Looking Back
Use: Skit or Puppet Show
Cast: (8) LOT's WIFE, DAUGHTERS (MIDRASH and AGGADAH)
2 SHOPKEEPERS (SOLOMON and SHOPKEEPER 2), GANG MEMBERS (LARRY, CURLY, and MOE)
Props: Cellphone, spice shop, many spice containers, box, sickle or wooden club weapon, 2nd shop products (wooden bowls and pots), shekels (coins)
Time: 8 minutes

(There is a market scene with two shops: SOLOMON's Spice Shop and another shop of random products such as wooden bowls and pots. LOT's WIFE and DAUGHTERS, MIDRASH and AGGADAH, approach a market scene. The GANG MEMBERS are at the side whispering among themselves, planning their next move. LOT's WIFE is doing a live video on her phone. SOLOMON is tending to his spice shop while SHOPKEEPER 2 is working in the other shop.)

LOT'S WIFE:	Hello, everyone. Lot's wife here. I'm doing a live here at the market in Sodom. My daughters, *(motions to DAUGHTERS)* Midrash and Aggadah . . . *(to the DAUGHTERS)* Say hello, girls.
DAUGHTERS:	*(Wave)* Hi!
LOT'S WIFE:	We are here at the market buying some spices.
MIDRASH:	Yeah, later on we'll be doing a cooking show for you guys, so you'll want to stay tuned for that.
AGGADAH:	What's the name of the dish we'll be making, Mom?
LOT'S WIFE:	We'll actually do two dishes: Salted Chicken and Sea Salt Cookies.
MIDRASH:	Mom loves her salt recipes. So yummy!

LOT'S WIFE: *(Speaking to the audience on the phone)* So, we're going to head on in to my favorite shop here at the market: Solomon's Spice Shop.

SOLOMON: Hello, how may I help you ladies?

LOT'S WIFE: Hi, Solomon, I'm back again showing my followers where I shop for my spices.

SOLOMON: *(Awkwardly waves at the phone)* Hello. Come on over, Mrs. Lot. I'll show you my assorted variety of spices.

LOT'S WIFE: No need, Solomon. Just take me to the salt section as usual.

MIDRASH: Goodness, Mom, you eat so much salt you're going to turn into salt.

LOT'S WIFE: *(To MIDRASH)* Very funny, my daughter. *(To the phone)* She's always making jokes.

(SOLOMON directs LOT's WIFE and DAUGHTERS to the salt section.)

SOLOMON: Here are all the salts: Sea salt, kosher salt, pickling salt, pink salt, garlic salt, flake salt, bath salts . . .

(LOT's WIFE greedily grabs one container after another.)

LOT'S WIFE: A girl can never have too much salt. *(To the audience on the phone)* See, guys, I told you he had all the good stuff.

(The GANG MEMBERS enter the spice shop and approach SOLOMON.)

LARRY: Give me all your shekels.

CURLY: *(Holds up his wooden club)* Don't make me whack your head.

MOE: Yeah, don't make him whack ya!

CURLY: *(Pushes MOE)* Hush!

SOLOMON: *(Pulls out a bigger wooden club)* Get out of here! *(Pushes them)*

(The GANG MEMBERS stumble but grab products as they run out. CURLY is brandishing the wooden club, and it makes the DAUGHTERS duck for cover. LOT's WIFE continues unfazed browsing through the salt varieties.)

LOT'S WIFE: *(To her DAUGHTERS)* Stop being dramatic, girls. You can't be scared of a bunch of stooges looking for some pocket money. Help me hold some of this. *(Hands some of the salt to her DAUGHTERS)*

SOLOMON: *(Straightens himself)* That's it. That's the last straw. I'm so sick of it here. Those hoodlums have been tormenting the shopkeepers for a long time. This city is getting worse and worse. I'm getting away from Sodom. *(Starts to box up his salts and other spices, even taking some from LOT's WIFE)*

LOT'S WIFE: Wait, I want to buy the salts. All of the salts. Where will you move to anyway, Solomon?

SOLOMON: I don't know. Maybe Gomorrah. I hear the weather is warmer over there.

LOT'S WIFE: Sodom . . Gomorrah . . . all the cities around here are the same.

MIDRASH: Yeah, the grass isn't always greener on the other side.

AGGADAH: But it probably is in Gomorrah. Isn't Gomorrah built over a cesspool? Green grass grows over cesspools. Just saying . . .

(The GANG MEMBERS rush back in this time to SHOPKEEPER 2.)

LARRY: Give me all your shekels.

SOLOMON:	I'm outta here. *(Picks up his box of spices, grabs a few more from LOT's WIFE, and runs away.)*

MIDRASH: Shouldn't we go, Mom? Shouldn't we leave the market, too? It's so dangerous. What if they come back and rob us, too?

LOT'S WIFE: Oh, we're fine. Those boys are just misguided youth. They aren't going to hurt anybody. *(To the phone)* OK, guys, I'm going to sign off for now. Tell me in the comments where you buy your salt. It looks like I need some recommendations. Bye-bye for now.

MIDRASH: Mom, Solomon had a point. The city is getting more and more dangerous.

LOT'S WIFE: Sodom is our home. It's a good place. It just needs a little rehabilitation. Just look back at all the good times we've had here.

AGGADAH: Yeah, all our friends are here.

MIDRASH: Maybe it's not a good thing to look back too much.

LOT'S WIFE: We aren't going to let a little crime and sin scare us away. Anytime I'm feeling bad about being here in this land of sin, I just look back at all the good times we've had here. Going to the PTA meetings, joining the quilting club. Looking back is fine.

(The three GANG MEMBERS walk behind LOT's WIFE. CURLY is slapping the wooden club against the palm of his hand.)

AGGADAH: *(Notices CURLY)* Mom, let's go home now.

LOT'S WIFE: No way, I just got started shopping. *(Starts to turn around)*

MIDRASH: Don't turn back.

(LOT's WIFE turns back toward the shop and is face-to-face with CURLY and the others.)

112

LOT'S WIFE: Midrash.

MIDRASH: Yes, Mom.

LOT'S WIFE: I think you were right. Looking back is not a good thing.

(LOT'S WIFE spins back around, grabs her DAUGHTERS, and runs out.)

                     Let's go!

(The GANG MEMBERS chase them out.)

LARRY: Give us some shekels.

Modern-Day Daniel

Topic: God's Protection

Use: Skit or Puppet Show

Cast: (14) 2 MEN, KING DARIUS, 2 GUARDS, DANIEL, 6 LIONS, GOD, 2 ANGELS (MICHAEL and ARIEL)

Props: Stone to cover LIONS' den, moon, sun, cellphone, Siri's previously recorded message, large stone, video call alert sound, staffs for the ANGELS

Time: 6 minutes

(DANIEL is on his knees with his hands in the prayer position in front of his face. Two MEN, two GUARDS, and KING DARIUS enter.)

MAN 1:   *(Gestures toward Daniel)* Here he is, King Darius.

MAN 2:   We told you he was defying your decree.

KING: Daniel, I ordered everyone in the kingdom not to pray to anyone but me. You disobeyed, Daniel. Guards, throw him in the lions' den. Daniel, I hope your God saves you.

(The GUARDS grab DANIEL, throw him in the LIONS' den, and move a stone to cover the entrance. The KING DARIUS, the GUARDS, and the two MEN exit. DANIEL picks himself up and looks around with his arms held out in front of him. The LIONS surround and approach him.)

DANIEL: *(In a stage whisper into his phone)* Siri, how can I save myself from a lion?

SIRI: *(Record SIRI's voice saying the following)* Hold your ground. If you see stalking indications, raise your arms above your head and shout.

(DANIEL obeys by waving his arms and shouting. The LIONS retreat momentarily.)

114

DANIEL: *(To SIRI)* Thank you, Siri. Guess I need to check in on InstaTwitFace so everyone will know where I am. *(Starts to type in location as a lion approaches from behind)* Daniel is in the lions' den.

(The LION roars, making DANIEL jump.)

Oh, brother, now they are hungry. *(Runs to the opposite side of the den)* Maybe I can order them some food and have it delivered. *(Scrolls through the phone)* Ahh, yes. Saul's Steak House. Perfect. I'll just order . . . *(Counts the lions)* One, two, three, four, five, six. *(Points to himself)* I'll order seven steaks, medium rare, with a side of fries for me.

(The LIONS roar again and get closer.)

On second thought, make that seven orders of fries and expedite it please. *(Clicks away on the phone)* And deliver to the lions' den on the outskirts of King Darius's palace. *(Pauses)* What? *(Grunts in anger as he reads)* "Sorry, we do not deliver to lions' dens." *(Puts the phone down)* Just wait until I write a review for your business.

(DANIEL sits down and puts his head in his hands. The LIONS start to sneak up behind him to attack.)

God, I know You are with me. Protect me from these lions. Your will be done.

(Two ANGELS—MICHAEL and ARIEL—appear holding staffs.)

MICHAEL: Do not fear, Daniel.

(DANIEL raises his head and stands up.)

ARIEL: God has heard your prayer. He sent us to shut the mouths of the lions.

DANIEL: Wow, thank you! Can I get a selfie with you guys? *(Starts to open his phone, but ARIEL shakes his head no and waves the phone away.)* OK, I understand. *(Puts his phone down)*

MICHAEL: Just rest. We will protect you for the night.

(The LIONS jump to attack. The ANGELS push them away two at a time. Two LIONS come back with mouths wide open, and the ANGELS shut their mouths.)

DANIEL: Well, it's getting late. You guys don't get tired, right?

ARIEL: We will be up all night. Don't worry.

DANIEL: *(Looks at his phone)* Would you guys happen to have a charger? *(The ANGELS shake their heads no.)* OK, I didn't think so. I'll go to sleep now. Good night.

ANGELS: Good night.

(DANIEL lies down on his side and puts his hands under his head. He falls asleep. The LIONS roar and try to approach. The two ANGELS stand ready with their staffs in front of their chests. Every now and then, the LIONS lunge, and the ANGELS must push them back. The moon lowers and the sun rises. KING DARIUS, the two GUARDS, and the two MEN reenter.)

MICHAEL: *(Taps DANIEL)* Daniel, wake up.

DANIEL: *(Yawns and stretches)* It feels like I just went to sleep.

ARIEL: We are leaving, Daniel. King Darius is here.

(The ANGELS exit. The GUARDS remove the stone from the den's entry.)

KING: Daniel, has your God saved you from the lions?

DANIEL: Yes, my God sent angels, and He shut the mouths of the lions.

(The GUARDS help DANIEL out of the den.)

KING: *(Examines DANIEL's arms)* The lions have not touched you. *(Looks at the MEN with contempt)* You two have done a very bad thing. You now will get what you wished for Daniel. Get into the lions' den.

(The GUARDS shove the MEN into the LIONS' den and move the stone. The LIONS attack the MEN.)

KING: *(Stands in front of the audience)* Today, I issue a new decree. Everyone must worship the God of Daniel. For He is the living God, and He endures forever. His kingdom will not be destroyed. He rescues and he saves. He performs signs and wonders. He has rescued Daniel from the lions. If you agree to follow my decree say, "Amen."

(Everyone exits.)

Modern-Day Lazarus

Topic: Jesus Heals
Use: Skit or Puppet Show
Cast: (7) LAZARUS, JESUS, MARTHA, MARY 1, SIRI (the phone app), MARY 2 (the mother of JESUS), CUSTOMER SERVICE AGENT
Props: Cellphone, video call alert sound, SIRI recorded messages
Time: 10 minutes

(LAZARUS lies dead inside the tomb. JESUS enters the scene, being led by MARTHA. MARY 1 stands up from her chair.)

MARTHA: Jesus, I know if you had been here, Lazarus wouldn't have died.

MARY 1:   *(Falls on her knees weeping)* We need Lazarus so much.

JESUS: *(Puts his face in his hands)* Lazarus was such a good friend to me. Where is he?

MARY 1:   *(Crying)* In the tomb. He's been dead for four days, Jesus.

MARTHA: Come, we will show you the tomb.

(MARTHA and MARY 1 take JESUS over to the tomb.)

MARY 1:   But don't go in there, Jesus. He's been dead so long he'll stink by now.

JESUS: Don't worry, Mary and Martha. *(Holds His hands out toward the tomb)* Lazarus, come forth!

(LAZARUS exits with grave clothes hanging off him. MARY 1 and MARTHA gasp, then shout for joy. They rush over to embrace LAZARUS. LAZARUS gazes at his hands in amazement.)

118

LAZARUS: Thank you, Jesus. I'm going to tell everyone of Your might and power! I can hardly contain myself. *(Jumps around worshipping God)*

(JESUS hugs LAZARUS, MARY 1, and MARTHA.)

JESUS: I must leave now. Trying times will come, but keep the faith.

MARTHA: We will, Jesus.

MARY 1:   Yes, we will keep the faith. There is no one like You!

(JESUS exits.)

LAZARUS: I have to tell everyone. I want to tell Jesus' mom first. *(Takes out his phone and speaks into it)* Hey, Siri, call Mary?

SIRI: OK, calling Mary Magdalene.

LAZARUS: No, Siri, not Mary Magdalene, Mary, the mother of Jesus.

SIRI: OK, calling Mary, the mother of Jesus. *(The phone rings, and voice mail picks up.)* Hello, you've reached . . .

MARY 2:   Mary, the mother of Jesus.

SIRI: Leave a message after the beep, and I will return your call. If you are calling to tell me that Jesus healed, saved, or delivered you, praise the Lord! *Beep.*

LAZARUS: Hi, Mary, it's me, Lazarus from Bethany. You know, the one who died a couple of days ago. I just wanted to tell you, Jesus brought me back to life. Praise the Lord! *(Clicks the phone off)* I'm so excited, I don't know what to do with myself. I think I'll post my testimony on InstaTicTwitFace.

MARTHA: Oh, sorry, Lazarus. There may be a problem. I changed your profile page to a memorial page since you passed away.

MARY 1: *(To LAZARUS)* You know how Martha always has to be doing something.

LAZARUS: It's OK, I'll just call and tell them I'm alive now and ask them to change it back. *(Starts to type on his phone while speaking)* What is the number for InstaTwitFace? *(Pauses)* OK, call. *(Phone rings.)*

AGENT: Hello. You have reached InstaTwitFace. How may I direct your call?

LAZARUS: Yes, ma'am, I died, and then my sister changed my profile page . . .

AGENT: Excuse me? Did you say you died?

LAZARUS: Well, yeah, but Jesus came by today and brought me back to life.

AGENT: *(Doubtful)* OK. . . .

LAZARUS: So I just need to change the page from a memorial page back to a normal page for a living person.

AGENT: OK, we can change that back. No problem. I just need you to answer the security questions. Tell me your name, please.

LAZARUS: I'm Lazarus from Bethany.

AGENT: Let me look that up. *(Pauses)* Yes. I found you. Your first security question: What is the first vehicle in which you ever rode?

LAZARUS: Oh, easy. We were all in one place and in one Accord.

AGENT: Accord. Yes, that's the correct answer. The second security question: What book of the Bible tells us that men are supposed to make the coffee?

LAZARUS: Hebrews. *(Elbows his sisters jokingly as he chuckles)* Get it? Hebrews. *He brews* the coffee. *(Laughs)*

AGENT: Yes, very good. OK, I just changed it back over to a personal profile page. Now we just need to change your username and password. What would you like for your new username?

LAZARUS: A new username? Let me see. How about "was dead"?

AGENT: Sorry, that username is already taken.

LAZARUS: How about "was dead2"?

AGENT: Sorry, that username is already taken.

MARTHA: Jesus has resurrected several people. Try a huge number.

LAZARUS: OK, try "was dead700."

AGENT: Yes, that will work. Now for the password.

LAZARUS: If my username is "was dead700," how about using "now alive" for my password.

AGENT: Sorry, you must use a number also.

LAZARUS: How about "now alive700"?

AGENT: Sorry, you must use a special character also.

LAZARUS: OK, "now alive700 exclamation point."

AGENT: Sorry, you must have a Bible verse in the password.

LAZARUS: OK, "now alive700 exclamation point Psalm 23."

AGENT: Sorry, you must perform an exercise while saying the password.

LAZARUS: You've got to be kidding me. *(Looks at MARTHA and MARY 1. They shrug.)* OK, "now alive700 exclamation point Psalm 23," and I'm spinning in a circle and then doing a jumping jack.

AGENT: I know you didn't move.

LAZARUS: *(Frustrated)* Ugghhh. *(Spins around and does one jumping jack)*

AGENT: Password accepted.

LAZARUS: Finally!

AGENT: Do you need help with anything else, sir?

LAZARUS: No, that'll be all. Thank you very much.

AGENT: Goodbye.

(LAZARUS starts typing on his phone.)

LAZARUS: OK, now let's open my page. There it is.

MARY 1:   If you don't mind, go on the Marketplace and see if anyone is selling spikenard. I want some nice-smelling perfume to anoint Jesus' feet the next time I see him. He's been so good to us. It's the least I can do. I'm so grateful.

LAZARUS: Yes, let me post my testimony real quick and I'll check out the Marketplace. *(Picks up his grave clothes and takes a selfie, then pretends to type)* "I'm baaaack! You can't keep a good man down when Jesus is around. This morning I was rotting in a tomb, but Jesus came by and I was alive by noon." And post!

MARY 1:   Rotting in a tomb, alive by noon. Now look on Marketplace and find me some perfume.

(LAZARUS scrolls on his phone.)

LAZARUS: Here's some nice-smelling spikenard. A guy named Barjonas has some for sale, but it's very expensive.

MARY 1:   *(Looks at LAZARUS' phone)* Jesus is worth it. And it says it's just a couple of miles away in Jerusalem. Let's go now before it gets dark.

LAZARUS: Yes, let's go. I can tell everyone on the way what Jesus did today.

(MARY 1, LAZARUS, and MARTHA exit laughing, talking, and holding close to one another.)

Modern-Day Jezebel

Topic: Covetousness
Use: Skit or Puppet Show
Cast: (5) QUEEN JEZEBEL, KING AHAB, NABOTH, 2 BAD DUDES
Props: Cellphone, video call alert sound, makeup brush, assorted pretend makeup
Time: 7 minutes

(NABOTH is on the right of the stage tending to his vineyard. KING AHAB and QUEEN JEZEBEL are in their palace on the left side of the stage. JEZEBEL is pretending to put on makeup in front of a mirror.)

JEZEBEL: Hi, guys, it's me, Queen Jezebel. *(Makes the hashtag sign with fingers)* Hashtag: Prettier than you. I thought since I'm a queen and everything, you guys would like to get a few makeup tips from me. I know you could never be as beautiful as I am, but it will give you something to which you can aspire. *(Makes the hashtag sign with fingers)* Hashtag: Living my best life.

(KING AHAB enters.)

AHAB: Hello, Jezebel, what are you up to today?

JEZEBEL: Oh, just talking to my followers. *(Makes the hashtag sign with fingers)* Hashtag: Half of the Kingdom follows me. I'm showing them how to be beautiful like a queen. What are you up to?

AHAB: *(Walks to the window and motions toward NABOTH)* I've been looking over there at Naboth's vineyard. Wouldn't that be a good spot for a vegetable garden?

JEZEBEL: Yes, dear, that would be perfect. *(Makes the hashtag sign with fingers)* Hashtag: I'm perfect.

AHAB: I wish it were mine.

JEZEBEL: You're the king. Go buy it from him.

AHAB: You think I should?

JEZEBEL: Go! Shoo! Let me finish my makeup tutorial.

AHAB: OK. *(Leaves and goes over to NABOTH's vineyard)*

JEZEBEL: Now back to my beauty. First, use this little brush to highlight your cheeks.

(KING AHAB approaches NABOTH.)

AHAB: Naboth, good morning.

NABOTH: Long live the king. *(Bows to KING AHAB)*

AHAB: Naboth, I was just thinking about starting a vegetable garden.

NABOTH: Yes, King Ahab, you would do great with a vegetable garden.

AHAB: Then it's settled. I'll buy this vineyard from you. How much do you want?

NABOTH: Oh, sorry, King Ahab, but this vineyard has been in the family for many years. I couldn't sell it.

AHAB: *(Jerks his body as if having a tantrum)* I'm going to tell my wife that you won't let me have the vineyard. *(Storms off back to JEZEBEL crying like a child)*

JEZEBEL: One little tip I would give you if you want to be as beautiful as a queen is to make your eyebrows connect like this. *(Draws a unibrow. Makes the hashtag sign with fingers)* Hashtag: Unibrows are life. Follow me for more beauty tips.

(KING AHAB lies down on his bed and turns his head to the wall. He kicks at the wall and jerks his body as if having a tantrum.)

JEZEBEL: Hold on, everyone. I think my husband is having a seizure. *(Walks over to AHAB)* Are you OK?

AHAB: *(Crying)* I asked Naboth if I could buy his vineyard, and he said no.

JEZEBEL: How can he say no to you? You're the king. You've always been a weak man. *(Makes the hashtag sign with fingers)* Hashtag: My husband is a crybaby. Well, I'll show Naboth. I'll write a bad review on his page. *(Scrolls on her phone)* Naboth's Vineyard. I'll leave a one-star review. There, that'll show him. *(Types on the phone as she leaves her review)* "Naboth is a horrible business owner. I went to his vineyard to get some grapes, and he was rude and disrespectful. I saw him kick a cat, and he almost kicked me."

AHAB: *(Turns to face JEZEBEL)* None of that happened.

JEZEBEL: *(Makes the hashtag sign with fingers)* Hashtag: Who cares!

AHAB: *(Jerks his body)* A bad review isn't going to get me what I want. I want the vineyard, Jezebel, and I can't have it.

JEZEBEL: You want the vineyard?

AHAB: *(Crying)* Yes, I want it.

JEZEBEL: Then you'll have it. *(Goes back over to her phone and speaks to it)* Sorry, guys, but I have some business I need to take care of. I'll have to end my livestream now. Take care of yourselves and remember: You'll never be as beautiful as me, but it doesn't hurt to try. Bye-bye now. *(Pushes a button on the phone)* OK, now for revenge. How dare Naboth make my husband cry like a little baby. *(Pauses)* I know what I can do! *(Grabs her phone and types. Makes the hashtag sign with fingers)* Hashtag: Get rid of my husband's problem and I'll pay you. Help wanted. I need a couple of bad dudes willing to do bad things in the city of Jezreel. Message me for details. *(The phone dings.)* Ohh, that was fast. *(Starts to type)* Thanks for answering my ad. Here's the plan. *(Types for a moment. Goes over to*

JEZEBEL: *the window and looks over at NABOTH's vineyard. The two BAD DUDES enter and each grab one of NABOTH's arms. They take him away.)* That'll teach you, Naboth. *(Goes over to KING AHAB)*

(KING AHAB turns over and looks at JEZEBEL.)

AHAB: I'm still so sad.

JEZEBEL: There's no need to be sad, Ahab. Naboth is gone. You are officially the owner of your very own vineyard. *(Makes the hashtag sign with fingers)* Hashtag: I took care of everything.

(KING AHAB jumps up.)

AHAB: Really? How?

(JEZEBEL runs her finger across her neck in a cutting motion.)

JEZEBEL: *(Makes the hashtag sign with fingers)* Hashtag: Naboth is history.

AHAB: *(Gasps and puts his hand over his mouth)* Jezebel, you are *(makes the hashtag sign with fingers)* hashtag: evil, but you get the job done.

JEZEBEL: Now, you need to take me out to dinner since I stole the vineyard for you.

(KING AHAB holds out his arm, and QUEEN JEZEBEL hooks her arm around his. They exit.)

Modern-Day Samson

Topic: God's Anointing
Use: Skit or Puppet Show
Cast: (4) SAMSON, DELILAH, CONSPIRATORS (GUY 1 and GUY 2)
Props: Cellphone, phone stand, light, video call alert sound, wig for SAMSON, 2 dumbbells, bowstrings, rope, strips of fabric, scissors
Time: 12 minutes

(SAMSON is wearing a long wig. He brushes back his hair with his hand. There is a cellphone and light set up to record a workout video and hair tutorial.)

SAMSON: *(Holding two dumbbells)* Hi, I'm Samson, and today is Man Crush Monday. I'm crushing on these muscles. *(Kisses his biceps and then starts curling the weights)* One and two and three. That's right. Lift those weights. Now higher. *(Starts to lift over his head)* One and two and three. These are the muscles that killed a lion and 3,000 Philistines. And just the other day, I picked up a gate, posts and all, and carried it all the way to the top of a hill.

(Two CONSPIRATORS and DELILAH peek in. The CONSPIRATORS motion toward SAMSON. DELILAH nods her head.)

DELILAH: That's him. That's Samson.

GUY 1: Look, this guy is horrible. He burned up our fields. He killed our men. He's just too strong.

GUY 2: Something suspicious is going on. Maybe he's drinking some kind of protein drink or something.

GUY 1: You find out how's he so strong and we'll give you 1,100 pieces of silver.

DELILAH: Eleven hundred pieces of silver? Wowee. *(Looks at Samson longingly)* But look, he's so cute. But that's a lot of silver. *(Holds up two hands as if balancing two items)* Samson or 1,100 pieces of silver? Hmm. I definitely choose the 1,100 pieces of silver. OK, count me in. I'll find out for you, don't worry.

GUY 2:   Don't let us down.

DELILAH: Don't worry. Just get the silver ready.

GUY 1:   *(To GUY 2)* Set up a GoFundMe account. I'm sure the other Philistines would like to donate to a worthy cause. Go!

(The CONSPIRATORS point again and push DELILAH in. She stumbles but regains her composure and approaches SAMSON. She looks back at the two CONSPIRATORS, and they motion toward SAMSON.)

DELILAH: Oh, Samson, look how strong you are.

SAMSON: *(Annoyed that DELILAH is interrupting his live video, he stage-whispers.)* I'm in the middle of a live video.

DELILAH: You're live? *(Steps in front of the camera)* Hello, everyone. I'm Delilah. *(Holds up the peace sign and makes a pose)*

(SAMSON pushes DELILAH away, and she flies across the room.)

                  My goodness, Samson. You don't realize how strong you are. You just about sent me flying out the window. *(She recovers and looks at the two CONSPIRATORS who motion her to go back to SAMSON.)*

SAMSON: I'm sorry, Delilah. You look very beautiful today.

DELILAH: *(Smiles bashfully)* Thank you, Samson. So, I was wondering, how are you so strong? If someone wanted to tie you up and capture you, what would they have to do?

SAMSON: Well, Delilah, that's an awfully suspicious question.

DELILAH: It's not suspicious. I ask all my strong friends that question.

SAMSON: Really? *(Squints his eyes suspiciously)* OK, well, if anyone ties me with seven fresh bowstrings that have not been dried, I'll become as weak as any other man.

(The two CONSPIRATORS rush out and reenter holding bowstrings.)

GUY 1:   *(Trying to get DELILAH's attention)* Psst. Psst.

(DELILAH looks over at them, and they wave her over. DELILAH walks backward and is quickly handed the bowstrings behind her back. She returns to SAMSON's side.)

DELILAH: *(Smiling coyly at SAMSON)* I have a surprise for you, Samson. Put down your weights, hold out your hands, and think about your favorite thing in the world.

SAMSON: *(Closes his eyes and holds out his hands)* OK. My favorite thing in the world? Let me think. Oh, I know. Honey from a lion's carcass.

DELILAH: *(Frowns as she starts to tie him up)* Honey from a lion's carcass. That's strange.

SAMSON: No, it's so sweet to see the carcass of something that tried to kill you, and when you realize God saved you from your enemy, it becomes a sweet memory.

DELILAH: *(Finishes and steps away. She motions for the CONSPIRATORS to come.)* OK, open your eyes.

(The two CONSPIRATORS rush over and grab hold of SAMSON, but he quickly snaps the bowstrings and bangs their heads together. They hold their heads and run off.)

SAMSON: Delilah, what did you do? *(Picks up the dumbbells and starts lifting them again. He goes over to the phone.)* The people in the comment section are saying you set me up.

DELILAH: You can't listen to everyone online. Believe me, it wasn't me. They must have been watching your livestream and heard it. Don't worry. They're gone. Look. *(Motions around the room. SAMSON looks around in the opposite direction and misses the two CONSPIRATORS reentering.)*

GUY 1:   *(Trying to get DELILAH's attention)* Psst. Psst.

(DELILAH turns to look at them. They raise their eyebrows and hold their palms up questioningly. DELILAH shrugs.)

DELILAH: You don't love me, Samson.

SAMSON: Why do you say that?

DELILAH: Because you don't tell me anything. You just lied to me.

SAMSON: But I don't tell anybody that. It could be dangerous.

DELILAH: Well, I guess we'll never get married then if you don't trust me.

SAMSON: Now, come on, Delilah. You know I love you and want to marry you. OK, I'll tell you, but I'm turning off my live video. I don't want anyone else to hear. *(Goes over to the phone and presses a button as if turning off the live video)* It's not bowstrings. If anyone ties me up with brand-new ropes that have never been used, I'll become as weak as any other man.

(DELILAH turns halfway toward the CONSPIRATORS and gives them a thumbs-up. They rush out and reenter holding a new rope. DELILAH backs over to them, and they hand it to her.)

DELILAH: Oh, Samson, thank you for trusting me. Hold out your hand and close your eyes. I may have found a wedding ring. I want to surprise you with something.

SAMSON: Really? *(Eagerly sets the weights down, closes his eyes, and holds out his hands with a smile on his face)* I'm so excited.

(DELILAH starts to tie up his hands with the new rope. The two CONSPIRATORS rush over and grab hold of SAMSON, but he quickly breaks free from the rope. He mimes punching the CONSPIRATORS, sending them flying away. SAMSON brushes off his arms and legs as he glares at DELILAH.)

                What in the world, Delilah?

DELILAH: What do you mean, Samson? I was right here with you. I didn't tell anyone anything, but I'm about to leave you forever. You have made a fool out of me. You don't trust me. We are over!

(DELILAH turns as if she is going to leave. SAMSON grabs her arm to stop her. The two CONSPIRATORS recuperate and hide again.)

SAMSON: No, don't leave, Delilah. I love you. OK. OK. I'll tell you. If you braid my hair and wrap it up with fabric, I'll become as weak as any other man.

DELILAH: *(Rolls her eyes)* Seriously? That doesn't even make sense. *(Turns to look at the CONSPIRATORS. They shrug and rush out. They reenter with strips of fabric. DELILAH backs up to them and takes the fabric.)*

SAMSON: Yes. It's true.

DELILAH: *(Sighs heavily as she sits down)* I'm losing my patience with you. Come and lay your head on my lap and close your eyes!

SAMSON: I don't know if I should.

DELILAH: Samson!

SAMSON: OK. OK. I'm coming.

(He lies down with his head in her lap.)

DELILAH: I want to recite a poem to you as I run my fingers through your hair.

SAMSON: OK.

DELILAH: Roses are red, *(She weaves the fabric into his hair.)*
Violets are blue,
The Philistines have come
To kill you.

(SAMSON's eyes spring open as the CONSPIRATORS grab him. SAMSON throws them out one by one. DELILAH crosses her arms.)

You do not trust me!

SAMSON: Well, Delilah, look at everything that has happened. You keep tying me up, and the Philistines keep appearing.

DELILAH: Why are you blaming me for that? It's not my fault what they do.

(SAMSON picks up his cellphone and starts tapping away.)

SAMSON: I'm going to conduct a poll to see if everyone thinks I'm overreacting. *(Taps away as he speaks)* Would you trust someone who almost had you killed three times?

DELILAH: OK, I'm leaving. *(Starts to walk away and gets to the CONSPIRATORS, who hold up a bag of money)*

SAMSON: Wait, Delilah. I'm sorry. I know it's not your fault what the Philistines do.

DELILAH: *(Turns and walks back to SAMSON. She sits down and motions him to come back over to her. He comes and puts his head back in her lap.)* You're right. I'm not the one who attacks you. You and I will never be close, because I know you don't trust me or love me. Tell me. Tell me. Tell me. Tell me. Tell me. Tell me.

SAMSON:　OK. If you stop asking, I will tell you. Look. No razor has ever been used on my head, because I have been a Nazirite dedicated to God from my mother's womb. If my head were shaved, my strength would leave me, and I would become as weak as any other man.

(The CONSPIRATORS rush out and reenter with scissors. They come up behind DELILAH and hand her the scissors. She quickly snips off some hair and pulls the wig off. The CONSPIRATORS rush to grab SAMSON. This time he does not fight back.)

DELILAH:　Give me the silver.

SAMSON:　You betrayed me for silver?

DELILAH:　Eleven hundred pieces of silver!

(The two CONSPIRATORS lead SAMSON away.)

I guess we aren't getting married. I guess he had to learn a lesson the hard way: If God gives you a special anointing, don't give that up for anyone.

PART THREE

MEDLEY OF HYMNS

The Me Medley

Topic: Selfishness
Use: Skit or Puppet Show
Cast: (3) TERRY, MARTY, ZOEY
Songs: "Standing in the Need of Prayer" (with adaptations), "God Is So Good" (with adaptations), "Do, Lord, Do Remember Me" (with adaptations)
Props: Three cellphones
Time: 8 minutes

(TERRY, MARTY, and ZOEY enter from different directions and greet each other enthusiastically. They hug, then quickly are engrossed in their phones. Their phones ring.)

TERRY:	*(Putting her phone to her ear)* Hello. *(Stands there nodding as if listening to a conversation)*
MARTY:	*(Pause)* Hi. Yes, this is Marty. I ordered the purse.
ZOEY	*(Pause)* No, I can't. I'm hanging out with my friends.
TERRY, MARTY & ZOEY:	*(Pause)* OK. Bye.
TERRY:	So, girls, are y'all ready to have fun?
MARTY & ZOEY:	Yes!
TERRY:	Good. Hold on for a minute, though. I want to take a selfie here. This is a great background.
MARTY & ZOEY:	Me too!

(All three start to take selfies.)

**TERRY, MARTY
& ZOEY:**   *(Sing to the tune of "Standing in the Need of Prayer")*
It's me, it's me, take a selfie,
Posing so beautifully.
It's me, it's me, take a selfie,
Looking so beautifully.

TERRY: Not my brother, not my sister, but it's me, O me,
The best in the family.
Not my brother, not my sister, but it's me, O me,
The best in the family.

**TERRY, MARTY
& ZOEY:**   It's me, it's me, take a selfie,
Posing so beautifully.
It's me, it's me, take a selfie,
Looking so beautifully.

TERRY: I got some great selfies.

**MARTY
& ZOEY:**   Me too!

TERRY: So, are you girls ready to have fun?

**MARTY
& ZOEY:**   Yes!

TERRY: Good. Hold on for a minute, though. I want to post this on my
InstaTwitFace.

**MARTY
& ZOEY:**   Me too!

(All three scroll on their phones as if posting their photos, then show their selfies to each other.)

TERRY:	Look at my selfie.
MARTY:	Nice, but check out mine. It's really good.
ZOEY:	Yeah, it's OK, but look at mine.

TERRY, MARTY & ZOEY:

(Sing to the tune of "God Is So Good")
I look so good,
I look so good,
I look so good,
I look so good to me.

TERRY:

(Sings as she is gazing at her selfie)
I could be a queen,
(MARTY and ZOEY look at TERRY and roll their eyes.)
I could be a queen,
I could be a queen,
I look so good to me.

MARTY:

(Sings as she is gazing at her selfie)
My pictures look pristine,
(TERRY and ZOEY look at MARTY and roll their eyes.)
My pictures look pristine,
My pictures look pristine,
I look so good to me.

ZOEY:

(Sings as she is gazing at her selfie)
Good looks are in my genes,
(TERRY and MARTY look at ZOEY and roll their eyes.)
Good looks are in my genes,
Good looks are in my genes,
I look so good to me.

TERRY:	There! My wonderful selfies are posted.
MARTY & ZOEY:	Mine, too!
TERRY:	Well, check out this friend suggestion. *(Shows her phone to MARTY and ZOEY)* Do you remember Sarah from middle school?
MARTY & ZOEY:	Yes, I know her, too.
MARTY:	Ask her if she remembers me.
ZOEY:	Ask her if she remembers me, too.
TERRY:	*(Sings to the tune of "Do, Lord, Do Remember Me" as he types)* Sarah, Sarah, do you remember me?
MARTY:	*(Sings to the tune of "Do, Lord, Do Remember Me" as she types)* Sarah, Sarah, do you remember me?
ZOEY:	*(Sings to the tune of "Do, Lord, Do Remember Me" as she types)* Sarah, Sarah, do you remember me?
TERRY, MARTY & ZOEY:	From back in middle school?
TERRY:	I'm sure she'll want to be my friend.
MARTY & ZOEY:	Yeah, me too.
TERRY:	Well, we've had a great time. I'd love to stay longer, but I have to go look at myself in the mirror for a while.
MARTY:	Yes, a wonderful time.

ZOEY: You know, I was thinking. Maybe next time, we can just hang out together without bringing our phones.

(TERRY, MARTY, and ZOEY are silent for a moment looking at one another and then burst out laughing.)

**TERRY &
MARTY:**   That's a good one, Zoey!

(ZOEY laughs.)

**TERRY &
MARTY:**   See you guys later! Bye!

(TERRY and MARTY exit first.)

ZOEY: I do wish we could talk to each other instead of playing on our phones. I miss my friends. *(Puts her head down and exits)*

Go Tell It Medley

Topic: Testify of God's Goodness

Use: Skit

Cast: (28+) CHOIR, MARY, JOSEPH, BABY JESUS, 3 ANGELS, ADULT JESUS, 2 GUARDS, 6 DISCIPLES including PETER, MODERN-DAY GRANDMA, 2 LITTLE GIRLS

Songs: "Tell Me the Story of Jesus," "I Love to Tell the Story," "Go Tell It on the Mountain" (with adaptations)

Props: Rocking chair, Bible, manger, blanket, podium, scroll, worktable, cross, sandpaper, tomb and large stone, "stones" to throw, white linen

Time: 10 minutes

(The CHOIR is center stage. A NATIVITY scene is to the right with MARY, JOSEPH, and BABY JESUS. Three ANGELS enter and stand behind the MARY and JOSEPH.)

(MODERN-DAY GRANDMA is sitting in a rocking chair to the left. Two LITTLE GIRLS come up and hand GRANDMA the Bible.)

CHOIR: *(Sings "Tell Me the Story of Jesus")*
Tell me the story of Jesus,
Write on my heart every word;
Tell me the story most precious,
(The ANGELS enter.)
Sweetest that ever was heard.
Tell how the angels in chorus,
Sang as they welcomed His birth,

ANGELS: "Glory to God in the highest!
Peace and good tidings to earth."

2 GIRLS: *(MARY picks up BABY JESUS. SHE, JOSEPH, and the ANGELS exit during the refrain.)*
Tell me the story of Jesus,

2 GIRLS: *(Continuing to sing "Tell Me the Story of Jesus")*
Write on my heart every word;
Tell me the story most precious,
Sweetest that ever was heard.

(ADULT JESUS comes on scene. He kneels. He prays in great turmoil. There is a worktable about 10 feet away. A cross and some sandpaper are on the worktable.)

CHOIR: *(Singing)* Fasting alone in the desert,
Tell of the days that are past,
How for our sins He was tempted,
Yet was triumphant at last.
(JESUS stands and starts to work, sanding the cross.)
Tell of the years of His labor,
Tell of the sorrow He bore;
He was despised and afflicted,
(Two GUARDS enter, hitting JESUS with a whip. MARY follows behind horrified.) Homeless, rejected, and poor.

2 GIRLS: *(The GUARDS quickly put JESUS on the cross during the chorus.)*
Tell me the story of Jesus,
Write on my heart every word;
(MARY approaches and falls to her knees.)
Tell me the story most precious,
Sweetest that ever was heard.
(JESUS bows His head in death.)

CHOIR: *(The GUARDS take JESUS down and lay Him flat, covering Him with white linen.)* Tell of the cross where they nailed Him,
Writhing in anguish and pain;
Tell of the grave where they laid Him,
(They roll a large stone in front of JESUS. A dejected MARY walk to the side and kneels.)
Tell how He liveth again.
(The stone opens, and JESUS steps out. MARY turns and comes running. She falls at His feet.) Love in that story so tender,

CHOIR: *(Continuing to sing "Tell Me the Story of Jesus")*
Clearer than ever I see;
Stay, let me weep while you whisper,

MARY: *(Singing)* "Love paid the ransom for me."

(The 6 DISCIPLES rush in while the two GIRLS and the CHOIR quietly hum the chorus. The DISCIPLES touch JESUS and look at His wounds.)

JESUS: *(Puts His hand on PETER's shoulder and speaks)* And I tell you that you are Peter, and upon this rock I will build My church; and the gates of hell shall not prevail against it. I will go away, but I will come again. While I am away, you must go into all the earth and preach the Gospel. *(JESUS points heavenward and exits.)*

CHOIR: Tell how He's gone back to heaven,
(MARY and the DISCIPLES gather in prayer.)
Up to the right hand of God,
How He is there interceding
While on this earth we must trod.
Tell of the sweet Holy Spirit
(All have their heads back looking upward with hands raised as they mouth words in prayer.)
He has poured out from above;
Tell how He's coming in glory
For all the saints who He loves.

2 GIRLS: *(They grab GRANDMA's hand and pull her to center stage as they sing.)*
Tell me the story of Jesus,
Write on my heart every word;
Tell me the story most precious,
Sweetest that ever was heard.

(TRANSITION: Music starts playing for "I Love to Tell the Story." Five DISCIPLES put up a podium, and PETER stands behind it with a scroll in his hand. He mimes preaching. The five DISCIPLES and MARY are sitting around listening. GRANDMA points to them as if showing them to the GIRLS.)

GRANDMA: *(Starts to sing "I Love to Tell the Story." PETER sings along softly while the DISCIPLES worship.)*

I love to tell the story of unseen things above:
of Jesus and His glory, of Jesus and His love.
I love to tell the story, because I know 'tis true.
It satisfies my longings as nothing else could do.
(GRANDMA exits with the GIRLS.)

CHOIR: *(Sing the chorus of "I Love to Tell the Story")*

I love to tell the story,
'Twill be my theme in glory,
To tell the old, old story
Of Jesus and His love.

(MARY stands. She walks over to the manger while singing as if she is reminiscing about the birth of JESUS. She picks up a blanket and holds it close.)

MARY: I love to tell the story. 'Tis pleasant to repeat
what seems, each time I tell it, more wonderfully sweet.
I love to tell the story, for some have never heard
the message of salvation from God's own holy Word.

CHOIR: *(Chorus)*

I love to tell the story,
'Twill be my theme in glory,
To tell the old, old story
Of Jesus and His love.

PETER: I love to tell the story, for those who know it best
Seem hungering and thirsting to hear it, like the rest.
And when, in scenes of glory, I sing the new, new song,
'Twill be the old, old story that I have loved so long.

CHOIR: *(Chorus)*

I love to tell the story,
'Twill be my theme in glory,
To tell the old, old story

CHOIR: *(Continuing to sing "I Love to Tell the Story")*
Of Jesus and His love.

PETER: *(Speaking to the DISCIPLES)* We must reach this world with this beautiful story of love and salvation. Go! Preach to the nations, telling them, "Repent, and be baptized every one of you in the name of Jesus Christ for the remission of sins, and ye shall receive the gift of the Holy Ghost."
(Sings to the tune of "Go Tell It on the Mountain")
Go, tell it on the mountain, *(He points to two DISCIPLES and points in front of the CHOIR. The two DISCIPLES go in the direction they were told to go. They stand in front of the CHOIR and mime preaching to the audience.)* Over the hills and everywhere;
Go, tell it on the mountain,
No matter what the cost.

CHOIR: The disciples went out preaching,
Baptizing one by one
(GUARDS enter and start beating the DISCIPLES while they continue preaching, then are carried away.)
In the name of Jesus.
They were beaten, hit, and scorned.

PETER: Go, tell it on the mountain,
(PETER points to two more DISCIPLES. They go as well and mime preaching to the audience.)
Over the hills and everywhere;
Go, tell it on the mountain,
No matter what the cost.

CHOIR: They preached the name of Jesus.
(GUARDS throw stones, and the DISCIPLES fall to the floor.)
The Holy Ghost fell down.
Tongues of fire all around them,
They were beaten to the ground.

PETER: *(Continuing to sing "Go Tell It on the Mountain")*
Go, tell it on the mountain,
*(PETER himself goes to the spot in front of the CHOIR and mimes
preaching..)* Over the hills and everywhere;
Go, tell it on the mountain,
No matter what the cost.

CHOIR: One by one we lost them.
*(GUARDS capture PETER. He is beaten and nailed to a cross upside
down but not lifted up.)*
Great men gave their all.
Many sinners still waiting.
Will you answer the great call?
(Sings acapella as everyone exits)
Go, tell it on the mountain,
Over the hills and everywhere;
Go, tell it on the mountain,
No matter what the cost.

Little People Used in Big Ways

Topic: God Uses the Willing

Use: Skit or Puppet Show

Cast: (21+) MORDECAI, ESTHER, HAMAN, 2 GUARDS, SINGERS, DAVID, JESSE, GOLIATH, DAVID'S 2 BROTHERS, 2 PHILISTINES, ZACCHAEUS, JESUS, PETER, JAMES, JOHN, PERSON 1, PERSON 2

Song: "Zacchaeus Was a Wee Little Man" (with adaptations)

Props: Throne, scroll, quill pen, sheep, leather bag containing bread, slingshot, stones, tree

Time: 8 minutes

(ESTHER is sitting on her throne. Two GUARDS are standing behind her. MORDECAI is standing next to her. HAMAN is sitting at the right of the stage holding a scroll and quill pen. He glares at MORDECAI and ESTHER, and on occasion, scribbles something on the scroll.)

MORDECAI:	Esther, *(motions toward HAMAN with his head)* Haman has an evil plan to kill all the Jews.
ESTHER:	*(Gasps)* Uncle Mordecai, I'm a Jew, too.
MORDECAI:	Now is the time to be brave, Esther. God is going to use you to save us all.
ESTHER:	Me? No, Uncle Mordecai, I'm a Jew and a woman.
MORDECAI:	Yes, you are, but the king will listen to you.
SINGERS:	*(Singing to the tune of "Zacchaeus Was a Wee Little Man")* Esther was a very brave girl, And a very brave girl was she. She came to the king's palace; It was her destiny. She foiled the plans of evil Haman.

(Two GUARDS enter and grab HAMAN.)

SINGERS: *(Speaking)* She said,

ESTHER: *(Continuing to sing "Zacchaeus Was a Wee Little Man" to HAMAN)* The fate you wished for the Jewish people will only happen to you.

SINGERS: *(Singing to HAMAN)* It will only happen to you.

(The GUARDS escort HAMAN out.)

MORDECAI: See, it doesn't matter your race or creed, God will use you.

(ESTHER puts her arm around MORDECAI, and they exit. DAVID enters with a sheep. JESSE approaches him with a leather bag containing bread.)

JESSE: David, check on your brothers and give them this food.

DAVID: Yes, Father.

(GOLIATH enters and stands center stage as DAVID approaches his two BROTHERS. DAVID hands his BROTHERS the bag with bread and moves closer to GOLIATH.)

GOLIATH: Cowards! You're all cowards. No one will come and fight me. *(Notices DAVID)* Ha! Surely they are not sending a little pipsqueak over here. I'll rip you to shreds and feed your flesh to the birds.

SINGERS: *(Singing to the tune of "Zacchaeus Was a Wee Little Man")*
David was a very little boy,
and a very little boy was he.
He came to give his big brothers some bread,
And the giant he wanted to see.
But the giant just mocked and shook his head. *(DAVID takes out his slingshot and picks up some stones.)*
(Speaking) David said,

DAVID: *(Continuing to sing to the tune of "Zacchaeus Was a Wee Little Man")* Goliath, you come with a spear and a roar,
But I come to you in the name of the Lord.

SINGERS: *(Singing)* But I come to you in the name of the Lord.

(DAVID swings the slingshot around and mimes firing a stone toward GOLIATH. GOLIATH grabs at his forehead, then stumbles backward and down to the ground. DAVID puts his foot on GOLIATH's chest.)

DAVID: *(Speaking)* I'm little, but my God is big!

(DAVID's two BROTHERS pat him on the back and usher him out as the two PHILISTINES carry GOLIATH out.)

(ZACCHAEUS rushes in among a throng of people, including JESUS, PETER, JAMES, and JOHN.)

ZACCHAEUS: *(Speaking)* Jesus? Where is Jesus? I want to see Him. *(Cranes his neck trying to see)* Where is He? *(Motions toward the tree)* I know. I'll climb that tree. *(Rushes to the tree and climbs it)* Yes, I see Him.

PERSON 1:   What are you doing up there, Zacchaeus? Get down.

PERSON 2:   You're a crooked tax collector. You should just get down and go home. No one wants you around.

ZACCHAEUS: I know who I am. I still want to see Jesus.

(JESUS approaches and looks up at ZACCHAEUS.)

JESUS: Zacchaeus, I know who you are also, and I want to go to your house today.

ZACCHAEUS: *(Points at himself)* Me?

SINGERS:	*(Sing to the tune of "Zacchaeus Was a Wee Little Man")* Zacchaeus was a wee little man, And a wee little man was he. He climbed up into a sycamore tree, For the Savior he wanted to see. And when the Savior passed that way, He looked up in the tree, *(Speaking)* and said,
JESUS:	*(Singing)* Now, Zacchaeus, you come down, For I'm coming to your house today.
SINGERS:	*(Singing)* For He's coming to your house today.

(ESTHER and DAVID reenter and join ZACCHAEUS to speak with JESUS.)

JESUS:	Boys and girls, as you can see, God can use you.
ESTHER:	It doesn't matter if you are black, white, brown, or yellow.
DAVID:	It doesn't matter if you are young or old.
ZACCHAEUS:	And it doesn't matter if you are short, tall, big, or small.
SINGERS:	*(Singing to the tune of "Zacchaeus Was a Wee Little Man")* You may be a very little child. A very little child you'll be. But God doesn't mind who you are; He wants to use everybody. No matter how old, how short or tall, You can join His family. (Speaking) He'll say,
JESUS:	*(Singing)* Come and follow Me. You can do a great work for Me.

(Everyone bows and exits.)

The Jesus Medley

Topic: Our Great God—An Easter Skit
Use: Skit
Cast: (25+) MARY 1, MARTHA, LAZARUS, GIRL, CHILDREN'S CHOIR, 4 MEN, PETER, JAMES, JOHN, 2 SOLDIERS, PILATE, MARY 2 (the mother of JESUS)
Songs: "Give Me Jesus," "Jesus Loves Me," "Jesus Is the Sweetest Name I Know," "Were You There?" "I'd Rather Have Jesus"
Props: Home of LAZARUS with rocking chair, bed, table, knitting, cup, teapot, small cloths for washing, sheet; resurrection scene with a cross; throne for PILATE
Time: 12 minutes

(On the left side of the stage is LAZARUS's house. LAZARUS is lying on his bed. There is a tomb on the stage where he will be buried. MARY 1 is sitting in a rocking chair knitting. There is an empty cup on a table next to her. MARTHA enters, opens a window, and moves around busily working in the kitchen. The right side of the stage is where the CHILDREN'S CHOIR will sing.)

MARY 1: Good morning, Martha.

MARTHA: Morning, Mary. *(Opens the window and peers out)* We had a long night with our sick brother, Lazarus. *(Takes a pot of tea over to MARY 1 and pours some into her cup.)*

MARY 1: We called for Jesus. Maybe He will come today.
(Starts to sing "Give Me Jesus")
In the morning when I rise,
In the morning when I rise,
In the morning when I rise,
Give me Jesus.
Give me Jesus, give me Jesus.
You may have all this world, give me Jesus.

(LAZARUS coughs, and MARY 1 rushes over to him. She picks up a cloth from the table and places it on his head.)

152

MARY 1:   *(Looks heavenward and speaks)* God, please touch our brother, Lazarus. *(Sings the second stanza of "Give Me Jesus" as MARTHA comes over)* Dark midnight was my cry,
Dark midnight was my cry,
Dark midnight was my cry,
Give me Jesus.
Give me Jesus, give me Jesus.
You may have all this world, give me Jesus.

LAZARUS: *(Coughs)* Don't worry about me, sisters. I know where I'm going when I die. *(Sings the fourth stanza of "Give Me Jesus" as his sisters attend to him)* Oh, when I come to die,
Oh, when I come to die,
Oh, when I come to die,
Give me Jesus.
Give me Jesus, give me Jesus.
You may have all this world, give me Jesus.

MARY 1 &
MARTHA: *(Sing the third stanza of "Give Me Jesus" as LAZARUS dies.)*
I heard the mourner say,
I heard the mourner say,
I heard the mourner say,
Give me Jesus.

MARTHA: Lazarus. Oh, Lazarus. He's gone, Mary.

(MARY 1 lays her head on her brother's chest.)

MARY 1 &
MARTHA: *(Sing the chorus of "Give Me Jesus" as they weep)*
Give me Jesus, give me Jesus.
You may have all this world, give me Jesus.

(The CHILDREN'S CHOIR enters. The GIRL leads, stands in front and sings as they move to their places to the right of the stage. While the CHILDREN sing, four MEN enter to view LAZARUS. MARY 1 and MARTHA wash LAZARUS and cover him with a sheet. The MEN carry LAZARUS to the tomb. MARY 1 and MARTHA follow behind, holding on to each other in grief.)

GIRL:	(Sings "Jesus Loves Me")
	Jesus loves me, this I know,
	For the Bible tells me so.
	Little ones to Him belong;
	They are weak, but He is strong.
	Yes, Jesus loves me.
	Yes, Jesus loves me.
	Yes, Jesus loves me.
	The Bible tells me so.

(JESUS enters and approaches MARY 1 and MARTHA. They hug Him and motion to the tomb. JESUS lowers His head and weeps silently. He walks over to the tomb.)

CHILDREN'S CHOIR:	Jesus loves me, this I know,
	For the Bible tells me so.
	Little ones to Him belong;
	(JESUS holds out His hand toward the tomb.)
	They are weak, but He is strong. *(The CHILDREN exit.)*

(LAZARUS walks out with the sheet hanging off. He tosses it away.)

LAZARUS:	(Sings) Yes, Jesus loves me.
	Yes, Jesus loves me.
	Yes, Jesus loves me.
	The Bible tells me so.

(MARY 1, MARTHA, and JESUS celebrate and hug each other and LAZARUS. PETER and JAMES enter and go to the right side of the stage and bow down to pray.)

JESUS:	I'm so happy for you, Lazarus.
LAZARUS:	Thank You, Jesus. I promise I will live for You and make my life matter for Your kingdom.
JESUS:	I know you will, Lazarus. I must go now to attend to some business.

(The music starts to play as JESUS moves to the right side of the stage. He bows down to pray with PETER, JAMES, and JOHN. MARY 1, MARTHA, and LAZARUS hug again.)

LAZARUS: *(Starts to sing "Jesus Is the Sweetest Name I Know")*
There have been names that I have loved to hear,
But never has there been a name so dear
To this heart of mine, as the name divine,
The precious, precious name of Jesus.

(Two SOLDIERS and PILATE enter. JESUS, PETER, JAMES, and JOHN stand up. During the chorus, PILATE points at JESUS. The SOLDIERS take JESUS and start beating him. PETER, JAMES, and JOHN distance themselves a bit and watch it all unfold.)

MARY 1,   *(Sing the chorus)*
MARTHA &   Jesus is the sweetest name I know,
LAZARUS: And He's just the same as His lovely name,
And that's the reason why I love Him so;
Oh, Jesus is the sweetest name I know.

LAZARUS: There is no name in earth or heav'n above,
That we should give such honor and such love
As the blessed name, let us all acclaim,
That wondrous, glorious name of Jesus.

(MARY 2, the mother of JESUS, rushes in. PETER, JAMES, and JOHN try to take her by the shoulders and guide her away, but she pulls away from them and stays.)

MARY 1,   *(Sing the chorus of "Jesus Is the Sweetest Name I Know")*
MARTHA &   Jesus is the sweetest name I know,
LAZARUS: And He's just the same as His lovely name,
And that's the reason why I love Him so;
Oh, Jesus is the sweetest name I know.

(The SOLDIERS take JESUS to the cross while MARY 2, the mother of JESUS, sings "Were You There?" PETER, JAMES, and JOHN bow their heads and walk away. PILATE goes to sit on his throne with his head in his hands.)

155

MARY 2:	Were you there when they crucified my Lord?
	Were you there when they crucified my Lord?
	Oh, sometimes it causes me to tremble, tremble, tremblc.
	Were you there when they crucified my Lord?

(The SOLDIERS mime nailing JESUS to the cross. JESUS bows His head in death.)

Were you there when they nailed Him to the tree?
Were you there when they nailed Him to the tree?
Oh, sometimes it causes me to tremble, tremble, tremble.
Were you there when they nailed Him to the tree?

(The SOLDIERS cover JESUS with a sheet and place Him in the tomb. PILATE and the SOLDIERS exit.)

Were you there when they laid Him in the tomb?
Were you there when they laid Him in the tomb?
Oh, sometimes it causes me to tremble, tremble, tremble.
Were you there when they laid Him in the tomb?

(Thunder sounds. Lights flash inside the tomb. JESUS exits with palms up and arms outstretched.)

MARY 2:	Were you there when God raised Him from the tomb?
	Were you there when God raised Him from the tomb?
	Oh, sometimes it causes me to tremble, tremble, tremble.
	Were you there when God raised Him from the tomb?

(MARY 1, MARTHA, LAZARUS, PETER, JAMES, JOHN, and the CHILDREN'S CHOIR all rush in to see JESUS. MARY 2 hugs JESUS. JOHN looks at JESUS' hands. The adults pat JESUS on the back and hug Him. The CHILDREN'S CHOIR take their places again to sing "I'd Rather Have Jesus.")

CHILDREN'S CHOIR:	I'd rather have Jesus than silver or gold,
	I'd rather be His than have riches untold;
	I'd rather have Jesus than houses or lands,
	I'd rather be led by His nail-pierced hand.

(PILATE comes back in and watches as he stands in front of his throne. He shakes his head and puts his hand on his forehead. PETER, JAMES, and JOHN join the CHILDREN'S CHOIR. The others remain with JESUS. He talks to them, pointing heavenward.)

PETER, JAMES & JOHN: *(Chorus)* Than to be the king of a vast domain
And be held in sin' dread sway.
 I'd rather have Jesus than anything
This world affords today.

CHILDREN'S CHOIR: I'd rather have Jesus than men's applause,
I'd rather be faithful to His dear cause;
I'd rather have Jesus than worldwide fame,
I'd rather be true to His holy name.

PETER, JAMES & JOHN: *(Chorus)* Than to be the king of a vast domain
And be held in sin's dread sway.
I'd rather have Jesus than anything
This world affords today.

(JESUS lifts his hands to heaven. MARY 1, MARTHA, LAZARUS, and MARY 2 all start to worship, raising their hands.)

CHILDREN'S CHOIR: He's fairer than lilies of rarest bloom,
He's sweeter than honey from out the comb;
He's all that my hungering spirit needs,
I'd rather have Jesus and let Him lead.

(JESUS motions for everyone to follow Him. They, except PILATE, follow JESUS out. PILATE shakes his head and exits alone.)

PETER, JAMES & JOHN: *(Chorus)* Than to be the king of a vast domain
And be held in sin's dread sway.
I'd rather have Jesus than anything
This world affords today.

Sources

Tabernacle and Temple Play References

Aleph Society. (2014, June 28). "Ta'anit 17a-b: Priestly Watches." Steinsaltz. https://steinsaltz.org/daf/taanit17

Barton, George A. "Temple of Herod." Jewish Encyclopedia. Accessed March 2, 2023. https://jewishencyclopedia.com/articles/14566-ulam

"A Day in the Life of the Holy Temple." Temple Institute. Accessed March 2, 2023. https://templeinstitute.org/a-day-in-the-life-of-the-holy-temple-introduction/

Evrah. (2016, March 30). "Temple 201—The Daily Tamid Service—Part 1." White Feather Ministries. https://whitefeatherministries.com/temple-201-the-daily-tamid-part-1/

Evrah. (2016, March 30). "Temple 201—The Daily Tamid Service—Part 2." White Feather Ministries. https://whitefeatherministries.com/temple-201-the-daily-tamid-service-part-2/

Evrah. (2016, April 2). "Temple 201—The Daily Tamid Service—Part 3." White Feather Ministries. https://whitefeatherministries.com/temple-201-the-daily-tamid-service-part-3/

Evrah. (2016, April 4). "Temple 201—The Daily Tamid Service—Part 4." White Feather Ministries. https://whitefeatherministries.com/temple-201-the-daily-tamid-service-part-4/

Gniwisch, Leibel. "The High Priest in Jewish Tradition." Chabad. Accessed March 2, 2023. https://www.chabad.org/library/article_cdo/aid/4195084/jewish/The-High-Priest-in-Jewish-Tradition.htm

Guggenheimer, Heinrich. "Jerusalem Talmud Shekalim 5:1," "Those Appointed to the Temple." Sefaria. Accessed March 2, 2023. https://www.sefaria.org/Jerusalem_Talmud_Shekalim.5.1.1?lang=bi

"Illustrated Tour of the Holy Temple." Temple Institute. https://templeinstitute.org/illustrated-tour-of-the-holy-temple-index/

Koren—Steinsaltz. "Mishnah Yoma 1:1," "The High Priest." Sefaria. Accessed March 2, 2023. https://www.sefaria.org/Mishnah_Yoma.1.1?ven=William_Davidson_Edition_-_English&lang=bi&with=all&lang2=en

Kulp, Joshua. "English Explanation of Mishnah Shekalim 5:1." White Feather Ministries. Accessed March 2, 2023. https://www.sefaria.org/English_Explanation_of_ Mishnah_Shekalim.5.1.1?ven=Mishnah_Yomit_by_Dr._Joshua_Kulp&lang=bi

McCrary, Dwayne. (2016, January 3). "The Shema and the Lord's Prayer." Explore the Bible. https://explorethebible.lifeway.com/blog/adults/the-shema-and-the-lords-prayer/

"Priestly Garments of the High Priest & Ordinary Priests." Temple Institute. Accessed March 2, 2023. https://templeinstitute.org/priestly-garments/

Shurpin, Yehuda. "How Were the Priests Divided?" Chabad. Accessed March 2, 2023. from https://www.chabad.org/library/article_cdo/aid/5585098/jewish/How-Were-the-Priests-Divided.htm

Shurpin, Yehuda. "The Levite Choir and Orchestra: What, Who and How?" Chabad. Accessed March 2, 2023. https://www.chabad.org/library/article_cdo/aid/ 5577273/jewish/The-Levite-Choir-and-Orchestra-What-Who-and-How.htm#:~: text=The%20following%20is%20a%20breakdown%20of%20the%20number,limi t%205%20There%20was%20only%20one%20cymbal%20used

Touger, Eliyahu, trans. "Mishneh Torah, Vessels of the Sanctuary and Those Who Serve Therein 7:1." Sefaria. Accessed March 2, 2023. https://www.sefaria.org/Mishneh_Torah%2C_Vessels_of_the_Sanctuary_and_Th ose_who_Serve_Therein.7.1?ven=Mishneh_Torah,_trans._by_Eliyahu_Touger._J erusalem,_Moznaim_Pub._c1986-c2007&lang=bi

Songs

The Tabernacle, the Temple and Me

Scene 1: Purification
"Wade in the Water" (African American Spiritual, Public Domain)
"Is Your All on the Altar?" (Written by E. A. Hoffman, Public Domain)

Scene 2: Miracles
"Jesus Is Here Right Now" (Written by Unknown, Public Domain), Adapted by Karen Jones

Scene 3: Trim Your Wick
"God Is So Good" (Written by Paul Makai, Traditional, Public Domain), Translated by Marilyn Foulkes, Adapted by Karen Jones
"I Need Thee Every Hour" (Written by Annie S. Hawks & Robert Lowry, Public Domain)

Scene 4: The Veil

> "I Surrender All" (Written by Judson W. Van De Venter, Public Domain), Adapted by Karen Jones

A Morning in the Temple

Scene 1: The House of Immersion

> "Whiter than Snow" (Written by James Nicholson, Public Domain), Adapted by Karen Jones

Scene 2: The Dawn Patrol

> "Farther Along" (Written by W. B. Stevens, Public Domain), Adapted by Karen Jones

Scene 4: The Holy Place

> "In the Sweet By and By" (Written by Sanford Fillmore Bennett, Public Domain), Adapted by Karen Jones

The Me Medley

> "Standing in the Need of Prayer" (African American Spiritual, Public Domain), Adapted by Karen Jones
>
> "God Is So Good" (Written by Paul Makai, Traditional, Public Domain), Adapted by Karen Jones
>
> "Do, Lord, Do Remember Me" (African American Spiritual, Public Domain), Adapted by Karen Jones

Go Tell It Medley

> "Tell Me the Story of Jesus" (Written by Adam Craig, Public Domain)
>
> "I Love to Tell the Story" (Written by Catherine Hankey, Public Domain)
>
> "Go Tell It on the Mountain" (Written by John W. Work, Jr., Public Domain), Adapted by Karen Jones

Little People Used in Big Ways

> "Zacchaeus Was a Wee Little Man" (Traditional, Public Domain), Adapted by Karen Jones

The Jesus Medley

> "Give Me Jesus" (African American Spiritual, Public Domain)
>
> "Jesus Loves Me" (Written by Anna B. Warner, Public Domain)
>
> "Jesus Is the Sweetest Name I Know" (Written by Lela B. Long, Public Domain)
>
> "Were You There?" (African American Spiritual, Public Domain)
>
> "I'd Rather Have Jesus" (Written by Rhea F. Miller, Public Domain)

Christian Skits & Puppet Shows Series

Clowns	Ark	Easter	Christmas	Temple
Grannies	Animals	Mother's	New	Tabernacle
Hillbillies	Angels	Day	Year's Day	Easter
	Toys	Father's	Thanksgiving	Bible
		Day		Characters

Black-Light-Compatible Skits & Puppet Shows

Creation	Pirates	Scientist	Cars	Royalty
Cowboys	Under the	Experiments	Trains	Rapunzel
Fables	Sea	Life	Diggers	Heaven
Christmas	Christmas	Lessons	Soldiers	Hell
Easter	Easter		Christmas	Christmas
			Easter	Easter

Available on Amazon

Like us on Facebook

PENTECOSTAL WARRIOR TRACTS

Journals, Sketch Books & Autograph Books

Fasting
Journal
&
Devotional

Books of
the
Bible
Journal

My
Pastor
Rocks
Autograph
Book

Acts 2:38
Journal &
Sketch
Book

Skirts,
Hair &
All the
Flair

I-54 Novelty Books

Jesus is
My
Superhero

You Rock!
Autograph
Book

Acts 2:38
Journal &
Sketch
Book

Prayer
Journal

Blank
Recipe
Book

Available on Amazon

Made in the USA
Columbia, SC
03 December 2024

48272916R00093